THE SECRET PARIS OF THE 30's

THE SECRET "PARIS OF THE 30's

BRASSAÏ

Translated from the French by
RICHARD MILLER

PANTHEON BOOKS, NEW YORK

Library of Congress Cataloging in Publication Data

Brassaï, Gyula Halász, called, 1899–

The Secret Paris of the 30's.

Translation of **Le Paris secret des années 30**.
   1. Paris—Social life and customs. 2. Paris—Description. I. Title.
DC715.B8213   1976   779′.9′9443610815   76-9976
ISBN 0-394-40841-1

Manufactured in the United States of America

DURING my first years in Paris, beginning in 1924, I lived at night, going to bed at sunrise, getting up at sunset, wandering about the city from Montparnasse to Montmartre. And even though I had always ignored and even disliked photography before, I was inspired to become a photographer by my desire to translate all the things that enchanted me in the nocturnal Paris I was experiencing. So **Paris de Nuit**, published in 1933, was born.

Sometimes I would be accompanied on my excursions by a friend or bodyguard. I strolled with Henry Miller through the XIIIth and XIVth arrondissements we both loved. On many evenings, Léon-Paul Fargue, the self-styled "Pedestrian of Paris," led me to discover the hidden areas of Ménilmontant, Belleville, Charonne, the Porte des Lilas, which he knew so well. I remember a late-night outing with Raymond Queneau, whom I took to a street dance in the suburbs. I also spent several nights in the neighborhoods around the Bassin de la Villette with Jacques Prévert, where we reveled in the "beauty of sinister things," as he used to call the pleasure those deserted quays, those desolate streets, that district of outcasts, crawling with tarts, full of warehouses and docks, gave us.

More often, however, I wandered alone in unsavory, ominous areas where I wouldn't dare go today. Sometimes, impelled by an inexplicable desire, I would even enter some dilapidated house, climb to the top of its dark stair-case, knock on a door and startle strangers awake, just to find out what unsuspected face Paris might show me from their window. This is how, once, around midnight, I got to photograph the street fair which had set up its merry-go-rounds, booths, its tiny circus, in the Place d'Italie. My intrusion frightened the inhabitants as much as my purpose: in those days, no one had heard of night photography. But oddly enough, doors were almost always opened to me, and I never got shot at, as might have happened, for disturbing a nocturnal household. I was hauled off to the police station by the patrol squad on only three occasions. The police refused to believe that anyone might want to take pictures by the canal at three A.M., and were more inclined to think I had been dumping a body into the greenish water. To show any possible interrogators it could be done, I usually carried with me some photographs I had taken at night.

Sometimes the inhabitants surprised me more than the view from their window could have. One winter's night, having spotted a seventh-story attic window in a decaying house across from the church of Saint-Séverin, I climbed the dark stairs, lit only by two small lamps. At the very top, I knocked on the last door. It swung open. A man and a women in nightgowns were standing in the middle of the small room, like the figures in Millet's **Angelus**. It was dark. Their somber, expressionless faces were lit by the faint reflection from the pink sky of Paris outside. "What do you want?" the man asked, without turning toward me. "I'd like to see Paris from your window. You'd be doing me a great favor." "I'm glad I can still do a favor for someone," he replied. "Go on, look . . . we don't know what it's like. We're both blind." I left, ashamed, heartsick. Two blind people living there, in that poor attic room! One could enter a dwelling at random and discover the strange, the tragic.

Just as night birds and nocturnal animals bring a forest to life when its daytime fauna fall silent and go to ground, so night in a large city brings out of its den an entire population that lives its life completely under cover of darkness. Some once-familiar figures in the army of night workers have disappeared: the repairers of the streetcar tracks, whose acetylene torches made fireworks, showers of violet sparks; the cesspool cleaners, who zealously pumped the septic tanks in the older neighborhoods; the porters and market gardeners, the agents, the butchers of La Villette, before Les Halles moved to Rungis.

The real night people, however, live at night not out of necessity, but because they want to. They belong to the world of pleasure, of love, vice, crime, drugs. A secret, suspicious world, closed to the uninitiated. Go at random into one of those seemingly ordinary bars in Montmartre, or into a dive in the Goutte-d'Or neighborhood. Nothing to show they are owned by clans of pimps, that they are often the scenes of bloody reckonings. Conversation ceases. The owner looks you over with an unfriendly glance. The clientele sizes you up: this intruder, this newcomer—is he an informer, a stool pigeon? Has he come in to blow the gig, to squeal? You may not be served, you may even be asked to leave, especially if you try to take pictures . . . And yet, drawn by the beauty of evil, the magic of the lower depths, having taken pictures for my "voyage to the end of night" from the outside, I wanted to know what went on inside, behind the walls, behind the façades, in the wings: bars, dives, night clubs, one-night hotels, bordellos, opium dens. I was eager to penetrate this other world, this fringe world, the secret, sinister world of mobsters, outcasts, toughs, pimps, whores, addicts, inverts. Rightly or wrongly, I felt at the time that this underground world represented Paris at its least cosmopolitan, at its most alive, its most authentic, that in these colorful faces of its underworld there had been preserved, from age to age, almost without alteration, the folklore of its most remote past.

The half-dressed girl strutting along the Rue des Lombards, picking up passers-by, murmurs the same "Want to come with me?" as the streetwalkers murmured to the rakes in the fourteenth century. She walks the same sidewalks as they did, the same pavement, stands on the same corners. The pimps, hatching shady deals and keeping a businesslike eye on their stables of girls, play endless games of cards or dice in the same cafés, the same cheap restaurants, as did the rogues of long ago, the **Coquillards** with whom François Villon hung out, or the companions of that other shady ex-convict, François-Eugène Vidocq, who became the chief of police.

Maybe my fascination with the underworld in those days was inspired by the infatuation with outcasts I had derived from some of my favorite writers: Stendhal, Mérimée, and above all Dostoevsky, Nietzsche. Enthralled by outlaws living outside the conventions, the rules, they admired their pride, their strength, their courage, their disdain for death. "Extraordinary men," wrote Dostoevsky in **The House of the Dead,** "perhaps the most richly endowed, the strongest of all our people. . . ." And let there be no mistake. The admiration expressed by the author of **Crime and Punishment** was not for revolutionary intellectuals or for political prisoners, but for real criminals: thieves, murderers, convicts—his own prison companions. These criminals cast out by society became his mentors, their doctrine of life—never written, but clear nonetheless—became his ideal. There was no pity in this. Dostoevsky consciously adopted the convicts' code: to live life according to one's own passions, to create one's own laws! Thus, more than a quarter of a century before Nietzsche, Raskolnikov had already removed himself "beyond good and evil." The author of **The Brothers Karamazov** admired these criminals so much that during his prison term he put up with the contempt with which they treated him. Was he not an outsider, a stool pigeon? "How is it," he wondered, "that they seemed then, they still seem, right to have despised me, and why is it that against my will I feel so weak, so insignificant, so—how terrible to say it—**ordinary,** compared to them?" For me too, or rather, for that other me of forty years ago, this infatuation for low places and shady young men was doubtless necessary. Could I otherwise have torn these few images from the strange Parisian nights of the thirties before they sank into nothingness? For me, fascination with a subject was always an indispensable stimulus.

To the present generation, some of these pictures will certainly seem as exotic as if they were of pygmies or Zulus. Even more so. This is because in our century's mad rush, style, morals, customs, art itself, have all been subjected to an unprecedented acceleration. Everything changes in a few years, and in a half-century everything has become far away, unrecognizable. Pierre Mac Orlan has already complained that nothing remained to testify to the experiences of his youth. "The almost total disappearance of everything picturesque," he wrote, "which formed the most touching part of life in 1900, is a fact." Raymond Queneau believes that these destroyed areas, these forgotten customs, live on in the work of the author of **Chant de l'équipage.** "This vanished world of hoods and underworld characters will take its place alongside the common folk and unscrupulous heroes of Petronius: time changes nothing. Any writer worthy of the name gives his era a certain image, at once true and poetic, lasting and evanescent; this is what Mac Orlan has done" (Preface to the Collected Works of Pierre Mac Orlan). Forty years ago, when I was planning the publication of the photographs in this book, I asked Pierre Mac Orlan to write the accompanying text. He came to Paris to meet me in a bistro near the Gare de l'Est. And he agreed with pleasure to write that text: my whores and crooks, my sailors, seemed to him to have come out of his own world. The collection was not published at that time. Now that the pictures are to appear accompanied by my own text, and not the one he wanted to write for me, I must include here a friendly thought for Pierre Mac Orlan.

In order to get into those suspicious, closed circles, so wary of witnesses, I had to employ both trickery and diplomacy. I usually tried to get friendly with someone who belonged. During the time a film was being made in a studio in Montmartre, I got acquainted with a young electrician, a member of the underworld. One evening, he took me to the Bal des Quatre Saisons in the Rue de Lappe. He introduced me to the owner, saying, "He's a friend." Not a word more. According to the custom and usage of the place, "friend" was like a password, a total guarantee. Having been introduced into one of the oldest and most authentic of the popular dance halls—no tourists, no bourgeois visitors among these toughs: hoods, thieves, small-time pimps—I hung out there for a time, just to make myself known and to become as invisible as possible. But it was very difficult to overcome their distrust of me. Despite the owner's acceptance, in the eyes of some of them I was still an informer. What I wanted was for the suggestion to take photographs not to seem to come from me, but from them. Having made a few friends among them, both men and women, I showed them my photographs, and finally I succeeded in getting what I wanted. For a couple of evenings I was allowed to work away without any trouble. Then suddenly . . . On that evening, the atmosphere was extraordinary. Such couples! Such faces! I worked in a kind of fever, sure that I was capturing the most wonderful underworld images. In those days, I was still using sheathed plates. My leather case held two dozen. Around midnight, I had only one unexposed plate left. I went to get it out of the bag, which I had left on a table. No bag. Stolen! Someone had lifted the whole take! The owner of the Quatre Saisons, his pride wounded, was more upset than I was. "That, to a friend!" He even put up a reward for whoever got back my bag, or turned in the thief. All in vain. I never found my leather bag, with its twenty-three marvelous, forever latent, images . . . It was probably tossed into a garbage can or into the gutter. And I understood: one never knew where one stood with these guys. They were capable of killing you for having taken their picture—most of them had reasons for protecting their anonymity, for staying unnoticed—or for having ignored them. All in all, I got out of that adventure rather well. They were very quick at settling scores! They could have ganged up on me with knives as I left the hall, instead of just stealing my twenty-three plates.

Photographing the girls and young toughs in the streets, in cafés, in whorehouses, I always ran the same risks. But my passion for capturing these pictures made me almost oblivious to danger. I escaped with a couple of pursuits and two broken cameras. The only time I was actually threatened with death was one morning when I was peacefully asleep in my hotel room. Someone knocked on the door. Waking with a start, I opened it. Before me stood a giant brandishing a crime magazine. I recognized him: a marvelous mobster I had photographed in a bar in the Saint-Merri quarter. He thrust a picture in the magazine under my nose. The caption, which had been added by the editors, read something like: "This murderer who . . . that murderer who . . ." "So I'm a murderer, am I?" he said, pulling his cap down over his forehead and brandishing a switchblade. "Then I'm going to kill you!" I was in bed, unarmed, in a real fix. I didn't even dare yell for fear of provoking him. What do you do when threatened with a knife? Luckily, I was able to wriggle out of it. Taking all my money, he left. My life had been spared. This experience still did not stop me from becoming linked one day with a gang from the Place d'Italie—"Big Albert's" gang. A huge strapping fellow, a gang leader, surrounded by six more or less colorless lieutenants who worshiped him unreservedly and obeyed him without scruple. This guy had three whores working for him. I accompanied them on some of their nighttime rambles. Although I succeeded in taking photographs of these toughs, one day they managed to lift my wallet, even though I had already paid them handsomely for their favors. I didn't lodge a complaint, however. Thievery for them, photographs for me. What they did was in character. To each his own.

THE CONCIERGE OF NOTRE DAME

ONE winter day in 1932, I got the urge to climb to the top of Notre Dame at night.

"The concierge is on the second floor," they told me at the entrance. So I climbed up—200 steps—and between two groups of tourists, I confronted the woman who watched over Notre Dame.

"Climb up here at night, sir? It's unheard of! It's out of the question. We're a national museum, just like the Louvre. And we close at five!"

I discreetly slipped her a bill.

"I shouldn't let you, sir! It's wrong! Even though I am very badly paid . . . and I have heart trouble, and I'm short of breath . . . Imagine! Two hundred steps every time I come up, and such steps! I was young once, not so fat, and I climbed up here twice a day. Now I come up in the morning and bring my lunch, and I don't go back down until evening . . . Coming up here twice in one day will be hard on me, very hard. But you're generous, and you love Notre

Dame! I'll do it for you . . . a favor I've never done for anyone else . . . Only promise me not to use any light, not even a match. We're right across from the Prefecture of Police. The slightest glimmer would be suspicious. I could lose my job over it . . ."

I reassured her. Taking advantage of a lull while the tourists moved off, the capacious woman continued in a low voice: "Look." With her plump finger, she indicated a particular place down in the square. "You see the third lamppost on the right? Be there at ten tonight. I don't want you to come looking for me in the concierge's loge."

I was under the lamppost on the stroke of ten, and through the November mist, I saw a voluminous silhouette emerge from the Rue du Cloître-Notre-Dame and come toward me.

"Follow me," the concierge whispered in a muffled voice.

We were like conspirators in a Victor Hugo novel. She carried a bunch of keys, and with them she opened the heavy door.

We climbed the spiral staircase. It was totally dark; the climb lasted an eternity. At last, we reached the open platform. Completely out of breath, my accomplice collapsed into her chair. Impatient, enraptured, I ran beside the balustrade. It was more beautiful than I had imagined! The dark, indefinable shapes were black as night, the fog over Paris was milk white! Scarcely discernible, the Hôtel-Dieu, the Tour Saint-Jacques, the Quartier Latin, the Sorbonne, were luminous and somber shapes . . . Paris was ageless, bodiless . . . Present and past, history and legend, intermingled. Atop this cathedral, I expected to meet Quasimodo the bell-ringer around some corner, and later, upon descending into the city, I would certainly pass Verlaine and François Villon, the Marquis de Sade, Gérard de Nerval, Restif de la Bretonne.

"It's marvelous, marvelous," I kept exclaiming to myself.

"Isn't it, sir?" the fat woman replied, brimming with pride at being the concierge of Notre Dame. "You don't see that anywhere else . . . We're at the heart of Paris . . . It beats the Eiffel Tower, doesn't it?"

But I had to get to the very top.

"Climb on up if you want, sir. I'll stay here; I can't go any farther . . . I trust you. Go on. You won't steal the towers of Notre Dame."

So up I climbed, still in complete darkness. I mounted the 378 steps. Coming out at the top, I saw behind the cathedral's spire the Seine glittering like a curved sword. Suddenly my foot brushed against something soft. I bent down, and beneath my fingers, numb from the cold of that November night, I felt the feathers of a dead pigeon. A dead pigeon, still warm . . .

Avenue de Neuilly. At this fair of fairs, there were all kinds of attractions: giant swings which produced screams and flying skirts; roller coasters, scenic railways, haunted castles, mysterious rivers, all those diabolical inventions to torture the body, to create exhilaration, fear, and . . . embracing couples in the friendly shadows.

The Foire du Trône gradually displaced the Foire de Neu-Neu. It was set up on the east, from the Place de la Nation to the Porte de Vincennes, along the Cours de Vincennes. In addition to the amusements, there were also food stalls with smoked ham, sausages, country bread, and the fair's great delicacy, gingerbread in the shape of hearts or piglets, the emblem of Saint Anthony. The Foire du Trône was driven out of Paris in its turn by the infernal traffic. Exiled to the Bois de Vincennes, it is almost the sole reminder of what the Parisian street fair was like forty years ago.

Conchita, or, Eros at the Street Fair

"Step right up, step right up! See beautiful girls! See it all! Step right up! Step right up!"

At the spring street fair in the Place d'Italie, out of a tent bearing the sign "Her Majesty, Woman," the girls appeared before the gathering crowd, dressed in their multicolored pajamas.

"Step right up, gentlemen. Unbelievably real **tableaux vivants!**" An enormously fat woman spoke into a megaphone, her voice harsh. "The Naked Idyll, Lesbos, the Naked Libertines, the Midnight Swim, Eve and the Snake, Diana the Huntress, and many more. Sensational, passionate, exciting. If you like flesh, if you like lovely bodies, if you like sex, you've got to see this! The best in the world!"

And the mistress of ceremonies—surely an ex-madam—her face blotched and puffy from alcohol, introduced them: "Mireille and her acrobatic dancing," "mysterious Bengalie in the famous belly dance," "Rose and her snake dance," Lydia, Charlotte, and finally—finally, "Her Majesty, Woman," "the young, the beautiful, the graceful Conchita . . ."

"Step right up, the show's starting . . ."

Out in the open, the girls gave a brief sample of their charms and talents.
The corps de ballet wasn't much, and neither was Conchita's dance. But her
graceful body, her breasts firm as those of a white Negress . . . To the nasal
sound of the phonograph, they bounced and thrust like the purple flowers on
the highest branches of paulownia trees. Men, mysteriously summoned, kept
arriving from every direction . . .

"Now, these ladies are going to undress and perform . . . For the small sum
of fifty francs, you can spend ten unforgettable minutes . . . Of course, the
show is forbidden to minors, but there's a special reduced price for our boys in
uniform . . . Step right up!"

Dressed in a transparent tunic, Conchita reappeared on the tiny stage, her
gorgeous breasts bathed in green, orange, and purple spotlights. It was worth
the money. She threw herself into her performance. Her flirtatious eyes
glittered below the spit-curls coquettishly stuck to her forehead; her glisten-
ing lips smiled. She would throw her head back now and then, close her
eyelids, and, her bosom heaving, she would stick the tip of her tongue out of
her half-open mouth. For those few seconds, Eros trod the vulgar boards. The
fat woman had told the truth, we had got our money's worth, and she was,
truly, "Her Majesty, Woman" . . .

So the booth where Conchita danced was never empty. Men milled around it as though under some kind of spell; some came out only to go in again, seeing every show until midnight. After the final turn, sailors, fliers, Zouaves, Alpine cavalrymen, firemen, waited for her at the exit . . . A crowd of escorts accompanied her to a café near the Place d'Italie. Conchita was in seventh heaven. In those spring days of 1933, she was a queen at the head of her army . . .

The Human Gorilla

A "Loïe Fuller" was dancing in a tent in the street fair in the Place d'Italie. A girl from the North, sad-faced and clear-eyed, with blond, wheat-colored hair. Her huge, winglike muslin veils were white, and under the colored spotlights they took on every color of the rainbow.

One evening when the curtain had fallen on the final performance of her "Artistic Vision" and the dancers had left the stage and gone into the wagon to dress, a lone man stayed behind in the tent, rocking a child in his arms. Timidly, he asked me the time, but I could feel he wanted to confide in me.

"I'm 'Loïe Fuller' 's husband," he said. "We live in Montmartre. We take the last subway home every night."

He was burly, as blond as his wife. He looked at me with his pale blue eyes. As for the golden-haired child asleep in his arms, it was like an angel by Fra Angelico.

"Once, my wife danced in music halls. That's where I met her. Let me introduce myself: I'm Torgues, the Human Gorilla."

Seeing my surprise, he explained, "You must have heard of me. I'm famous. I did the stunts for Douglas Fairbanks in Hollywood and for Harry Piel in Germany. And I invented my own act . . . When I was dressed as a gorilla, everyone took me for the real thing . . . But . . . well, right now, I'm out of work . . . For weeks now I haven't been able to pay our hotel bill. So my wife is dancing here, every night until midnight, for eighteen francs."

"Eighteen francs," I said, astonished. "But the subway trip already costs half that . . ."

"True, but with what's left over we can buy milk for little Peter . . . We're living on bread and milk ourselves . . ."

One day, I visited them in Montmartre. They were living in a hotel for acrobats not far from the Cirque Médrano. Everyone there was either a magician, a trapeze artist, or a snake charmer. While I was looking for their

room, I mistook the door. And there I saw an unforgettable sight: a man was standing on his head between the gas heater and the bidet, his legs in the air, his skull, smooth as an ostrich egg, balanced on a carafe. With great presence of mind, and still balancing on his head, he directed me to the Human Gorilla.

In my honor, and to the great delight of his son—barely sixteen months old, Peterchen himself could already do a complete backbend and a few other stunts—the Human Gorilla unpacked his voluminous costume and transformed himself before my eyes. Had I not known who was concealed beneath that skin, I would have been frightened. It was easy to imagine the attraction of his act: the animal climbing with ease up to the roof of the circus tent, swinging among the beams and ropes.

An album stuffed with photographs displayed his feats in the ring, and also outside it, climbing factory chimneys, church steeples, bridges, viaducts . . . There were other photos of Torgues leaping into an automobile from a moving train, tumbling from a plane onto a locomotive, accomplishing unbelievably dangerous jumps. He could climb any building with the same disconcerting ease, solely by the strength in his arms and fingers, gripping hold of the slightest outcropping . . .

Because his papers were not in order, however, this king of acrobats had to turn down all the offers that kept coming in from the biggest circuses and music halls all over the world. The Germans—he was German, as was "Loïe Fuller"—considered him a deserter and refused to give him a passport. This was in the early days of Nazism.

Then one day Paramount, unaware of his situation, sent him a ticket to Hollywood. Torgues wanted to try his luck no matter what. I don't know how, but without passport or visa he set out for America, leaving his wife and child destitute in Paris.

At Ellis Island, he jumped off the boat into the Hudson River and attempted to swim to the city. The river police chased him, fished him out, and turned him over to the German authorities, who put him back on board a ship to return him to his own country. He was put in the brig and warned that at the least attempt to escape he would be shot. But as the English coast came into view, Torgues escaped from his irons, broke down the door to the brig, and jumped off the German steamer into the ocean, swimming to England . . .

He described his trip to me as though relating a short outing to the suburbs . . . His letter was cheerful and full of optimism. It came from England, written from his cell, postmarked Brighton Prison.

THE LAST BUM OF THE COUR DES MIRACLES

DURING my nocturnal excursions, while strolling beneath the bridges along the Seine, I would often come upon weird piles of crates, boxes, sacks stuffed with paper and rags. Was it some treasure hidden by clandestine ragpickers? One evening, however, on the Quai des Orfèvres, beneath the arches of the Pont-Neuf, I was astonished to see a live, human face emerge from beneath a pile of rags. And what a face! It was swollen, covered with sores and bumps, the face of a Cro-Magnon goddess. No sooner had it appeared than it disappeared again behind the scraps of rubbish. Then another head appeared, more human, with a tousled beard. The creature arose from his litter. He muttered wary threats and insults at me. But seeing that I was neither a cop nor a stool pigeon, he soon became more friendly.

When my eyes had grown accustomed to the darkness, I saw that what I had mistaken for a garbage heap was a kind of dwelling. The stacked crates and sacks created a rampart against intruders, and against the wind which blew lustily through the arches of the bridge.

"Buy me a liter of wine and I'll bring my darling out." I agreed to the deal without being sure whether his darling was his wife or his cat. And I offered him a couple of packs of cigarettes.

"Are you the one who had the fire last night?" I asked him. I had seen it from the end of the Vert-Galant.

"Yes, that was me," he replied. "We cook up something every evening around seven. If you come back tomorrow, you can take our picture around the fire . . . I was rude to you . . . But I've got to be careful. Cops, stoolies . . . They can get us chased out of here . . . I've already been picked up by the cops once; they took us off to God knows where, maybe it was Nanterre . . . they even made us take a bath. A real bunch of animals, a bunch of dopes. Don't they know that in winter the dirt keeps out the cold, the bad weather. Fortunately we got away and came back here. There's nothing like the quays along the Seine . . ."

I kept my appointment the next evening at the time he had told me. My bum and his companion were cooking. Some blackish substance was simmering in a rusty pot, set over the flames of a wood fire. The woman scurried off as I approached.

"Doudou's afraid of strangers . . . You understand. It's something she can't control . . . She's a wild one, but she's okay. Doudou, come on back!"

He called in vain.

"We've been living here for four months," the fellow told me, stoking up the dying, smoking fire with some damp branches. "At first we lived on the quays across the way. But we got chased out of there by the floods . . . That was really something! The water rose very suddenly one night. We couldn't even save our stuff. We just ran up the stairs. I thought we'd lost everything, our sacks, our cooking things, the baby carriage, our cartons, our other clothes . . . But Doudou pulled her skirt up high and waded back and forth through the freezing water a dozen times . . . She was able to save all our stuff . . . What a woman! She's got courage. There's no one like her! Thanks to her, everything was saved. And it wasn't easy, believe me, what with the water rising. It almost knocked her over and carried her off . . . my dove."

I looked at the old beggar's face. Neither alcohol nor the nearly bestial life he led had succeeded in brutalizing him. He was full of good spirits, and his

eyes sparkled with mischief and intelligence. And how well he turned a phrase, with what tenderness he referred to his filthy companion: Doudou, my dove . . .

"Society didn't want anything to do with me," he said philosophically, "and I didn't want anything to do with it. I made my choice . . . and I've got my independence."

"But isn't it awfully hard for you to spend the night under the bridges, in all kinds of weather?"

"A question of habit," he replied. "And Doudou's wonderful! She's at Les Halles for food every morning at five o'clock. It's not always first class," and he chuckled in his beard, "but we always have something to keep from starving. Wine's a bigger problem. Don't ask how I get it, that's my secret . . . I can't tell you everything, after all . . ."

He laughed again and poked the fire. As for Doudou, she remained hidden behind the crates, in her boudoir. Instead, I saw a tiny black cat emerge from beneath the sacking. "Minette isn't as wild; she'll even let you pet her." She had her own personal hideout between the two bums, beneath the warm rags.

"Of course, you have the public soup kitchens, the Salvation Army, the bistros in Les Halles, at the Place Maubert. Not for me! I could go to Roger, at La Grenouille in the Rue des Grands-Augustins, too . . . He gives away soup every evening to the gang. He's not dumb! He knows how to get free publicity for his restaurant! An article here, a photograph there: 'Roger the Magnanimous, Roger the Generous, Roger the Bums' Benefactor!' He wallpapers his restaurant with these great notices and brings in customers, hobo-lovers, crook-lovers . . . I'd rather be fed by Doudou and make my own soup in the evening . . ."

As I took leave of them, I noticed a rusty, broken-down baby carriage. It was "garaged" between the crates. This, without a doubt, is the most desirable and precious of a bum's possessions.

"See, that's our market wagon. Come back tomorrow, I'm inviting you. For dinner, we'll have sausage, herring, all the wine you can drink . . ."

The Cours des Miracles—courts of miracles—have existed in Paris since the Middle Ages. Springing up on the waste land beyond the suburbs, they attracted all the miserable cripples, the down-and-out, beggars, vagabonds, thieves, bandits, disbanded mercenaries, the whole population of the ragged, the tattered, and the hungry which society had cast out. Even the police dared not go into these havens for outlaws for fear of being killed. Where did the name come from? Among these vagrants, there were many fakers. During the day, they would exhibit their infirmities, begging for alms, but when evening came, their bodies would grow straight—the daily "miracle"—their eyesight would return, their crooked backs would disappear, and they could walk and run without crutches, without canes, abandoning themselves to drink, revelry, debauchery. The largest of the Cours des Miracles, known as the Grande Truanderie—the Thieves' Palace—was located north of Les Halles, between the Rue Montorgueil, the Rue Saint-Denis, and the Rue Saint-Sauveur. The dregs of the capital—a tenth of the population—was crammed into this filthy, muddy, stinking ghetto. "A hideous wart on the face of Paris," wrote Victor Hugo, but a wart that the "City of Light" succeeded in concealing from its noble visitors.

The Thieves' Palace did not survive the first half of the seventeenth century. La Reynie, the infamous lieutenant of police, in his determination to clean up Paris, removed the "wart." The whole of this picturesque populace—the inspiration of Jacques Caillot—was pursued by the militia and dispersed. The crooks and bandits separated off from the vagabonds and the beggars to form what gradually became known as the "underworld." The sick, invalids, cripples, were taken into hospices and old-age homes. As for the hordes of beggars, they crossed to the other side of the Boulevard Sébastopol and took over the labyrinth of alleys in the old Beaubourg quarter: the Rue de Venise, the Impasse Clairvaux, the Rue Brantôme, the Rue du Maure, and so on. When this area was eventually partly torn down, the remains of the Cour des Miracles migrated to the Saint-Paul quarter and then over to the Left Bank.

Paris still had around 12,000 **clochards**, or bums, in the thirties. Their principal strongholds were the Rue Saint-Séverin, the Rue de la Huchette, Rue de la Harpe, the Rue Mouffetard, the Montagne-Saint-Geneviève, the

Place Maubert. Some bistros and even some hotels, like the Petit Bacchus in the Rue de la Harpe, the Belle Etoile in the Rue Xavier-Privas, welcomed the vagabonds, the down-and-out, the ragpickers. The most picturesque and hospitable of these havens for outcasts was a bistro at the corner of the Rue Lagrange and the Place Maubert which was a regular flophouse; night and day, men and women in rags, sacks slung over their shoulders, would crowd around its counter. They drank cheap red wine straight from the bottle, ate soup out of tin cans, and weighed the cigarette butts they had picked up during the day which the owner bought from them. On the bistro's tiled floor and on the sidewalks outside, drowned in alcoholic fumes, other bums lay dozing. These poor souls, snoring and dreaming, could sleep the sleep of the just for twenty-four hours at a stretch, indifferent to the noise, the smoke, the cold, the heat, passers-by, and the roar of the traffic.

But the favorite spot for **clochards** was naturally the banks of the Seine. Under the Pont-Neuf, the Pont du Carrousel, the Pont de Solférino, on the Quai des Fleurs and the Quai Montebello, there they felt at home. To awake at dawn beside the Seine to the sounds of the birds and roosters in the seed stores along the Quai de la Mégisserie, to enjoy the sunrise behind Notre Dame and the sunset behind the Grand Palais or the Trocadéro, was the envied privilege this group, officially listed as S.D.F.—**sans domicile fixe,** without permanent residence—enjoyed, since they had sacrificed everything for their freedom.

Alas! the **clochard's** profession is becoming increasingly difficult, and the struggle for day-to-day survival is an heroic undertaking. Their number shrinks from year to year, like Balzac's **Peau de Chagrin.** Four years ago, there were 5,000 of them—not even two-thousandths of the population—today there are only 2,000. And these last Parisian bums are being hunted down on all sides. The **dolce vita** is over and gone forever. A place to sleep and food to eat are problems that have become more and more impossible for them to solve. The supermarkets that are gradually replacing the open markets are forbidden to them; the transfer of Les Halles to Rungis has deprived them of their main source of supply. The demolition of the last twisted alleys in the old quarters, construction on the last remaining open terrain, has driven them from their lairs, just as the superhighways along the Seine have dislodged them from beneath the bridges. With the last of the **clochards** an age-old family is being wiped out. And in Paris, no one gives a thought to keeping them, setting up reservations for tramps and outlaws, as America did for the last of the Mohicans and Apaches. Yet by and large, the Parisian **clochards** had a humanity, they mocked everything with good humor, with stoicism, they laughed at it all from behind their bushy beards. The knell is sounding for these last survivors of the Cour des Miracles. We can mourn or we can rejoice, but one thing is true: their disappearance will erase from Parisian folklore one of the delectable things that went to make up its charm.

A NIGHT WITH THE CESSPOOL CLEANERS

ONE of the more pungent aspects of nights in Paris in the thirties was the anachronistic presence of the Ancient Guild of Cesspool Cleaners. How often—and in the memory of how many foreign visitors—the nocturnal charm of what was then called "Gay Paree" would be suddenly ruined by the flood of nauseating smells which would stink up the old quarters of Paris between midnight and dawn. Montmartre, Montparnasse, the Quartier Latin—none was spared. And this in the capital of a country reputed for the variety and excellence of its perfumes! For a long time, the new sewers which had been voted in decades before remained the privilege of posh neighborhoods. There were doubtless powerful interests at play. In spite of the law, there were still thousands of cesspools, and the cleaning industry was one of the most lucrative: it was the only one that didn't have to buy its raw material, and the only one that earned money at both ends, collecting and selling the same thing.

The arrival of the cesspool cleaners was far from subtle. Several macabre wagons drawn by white horses would advance in a lugubrious column through the narrow streets, and the squeak of the axles, the creak of the wheels, and the clatter of iron-shod hoofs on the cobblestones would jar the sleeping citizens awake. If, by some misfortune, the house to be treated was on your street, you would hear the shouts of the workers as they attached the pipes, and the noise of the air-pump motor, known as a "Richer pump" after its inventor, but familiarly called a "shit pump."

I decided I wanted to spend a night with the cesspool cleaners. I contacted them and I found my cicerone in the person of the driver of an "accessories" wagon.

"Be at the Rue Rambuteau tomorrow at midnight, at the corner of the Rue du Renard. We're cleaning a tenement, and it'll take a long time . . . You'll be able to take pictures . . ."

I shall never forget that driver's face. His nose was swollen with growths of flesh which nearly concealed his eyes, and he looked like the preacher painted by Ghirlandaio in the Louvre.

When we arrived on the site, near Les Halles, the Richer pump was already chugging away, throwing clouds of white vapor to the starry sky. Long hoses, attached one to the other, emerged from the main entrance of the building and lay coiled on the damp pavement; they met at a high cylindrical tank on four wheels. We were overcome by the suffocating odor. Oddly enough, however, it soon lost its excremental character and became more of an industrial odor, like ammonia. Shouting over the motor's din, my cicerone with the deformed nose explained the procedure to me: "The shit comes up through the pipe all on its own. The pump creates a vacuum, then the air pressure drives it into the tank."

Before setting out on this memorable evening, I had made a speech to my young assistant: "Control yourself, Robert! It's a job, like any other, although not a very desirable one. Don't make any pejorative remarks." But Robert never stopped exclaiming, "Oh, how it stinks, how it stinks! What a filthy way to make a living!"

One by one, the tank carts, drawn by slow-moving horses, were loaded with their cargo, rattled off down to the Seine, emptied it into a specially equipped barge, and returned. This shuttle went on throughout the night.

It was nearly two in the morning before the first job was completed. With a handkerchief pressed to my nose, I approached the cesspool. At the bottom, which was lit only by an electric bulb, a cleaner in rubber boots was sloshing around in the gooey pulp. He held the nozzle of the hose in both hands, and was directing it into every corner like a housewife with a vacuum cleaner.

"Toward the end," my guide informed me, "the hose can't draw alone. It has to be held and guided. But it's pretty dangerous. It's hydrogen sulfate! You can be asphyxiated in seconds, it can even explode! Whoever goes down in the tank risks his life every time. Lucky for him he gets double pay!"

The hoses with their iron rings were being disconnected and loaded onto the cart with fiendish speed. The only other occasion on which I have seen such rapidity was with traveling circus people striking their tents. And since the column was starting off for another destination, I—along with Robert, who was still complaining—climbed onto the accessory cart alongside our driver.

"Why did you tell me the other day that the Rue Rambuteau would be a long job?" I asked him.

"Because that building has very low-grade shit."

Who would have thought that this substance could have different "qualities," I wondered, amazed. But the driver soon gave me the reasons.

"I'll explain. In houses were there are people living, there's cooking, dishwashing, laundry, bathrooms, lots of water running. So the cesspool is easy to pump out. But in office buildings, the shit is harder, of course . . . So we have to pour a lot of water in, and mix it all together, before we can pump it out . . ."

After two houses in the Marais, which took a short time to clean, the column stopped somewhere in the Saint-Paul quarter in front of a bistro that was still open at that late hour. I learned that this was a bar reserved especially for cesspool cleaners, it was their "Maxim's." Every night, these virtuosi of the pump would break off their labors to come here to eat! And suddenly, the anonymous black-hooded and booted devils I had seen working away in the dark, hoisting up lead and stone covers from cesspools and

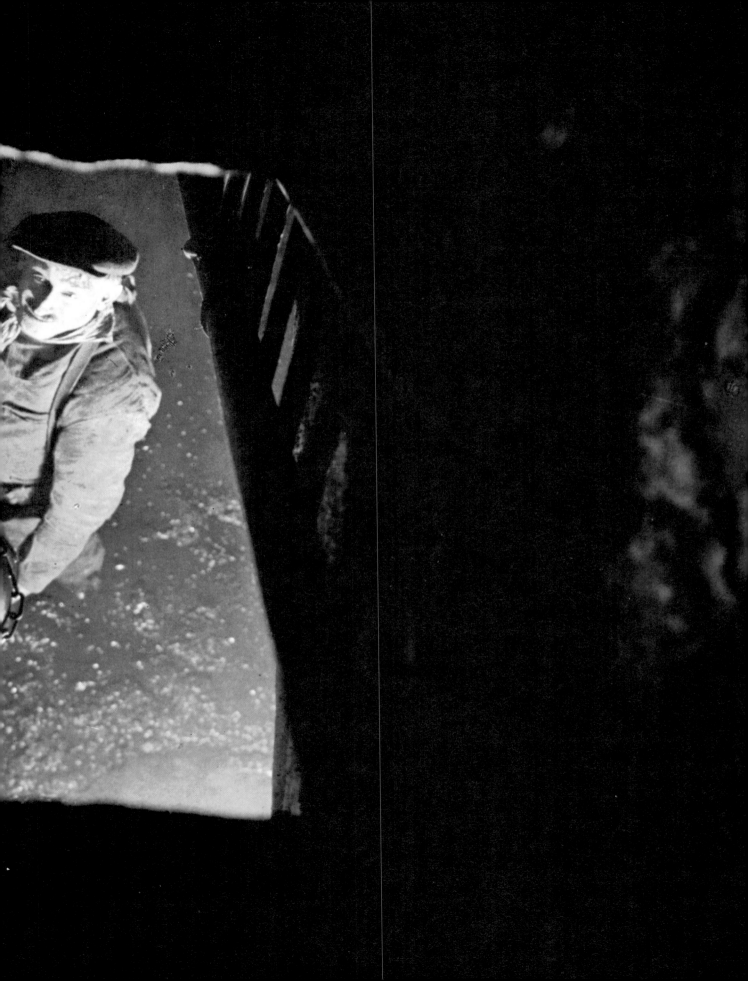

shoving down the hose, regained their human aspect. Almost all of them sported mustaches and extraordinary haircuts. They dug into their meal of cheese and sausages with great gusto, not even bothering to wash their hands, and swilled great gulps of the cheap wine the patron served. Having made friends, we were their guests; Robert, however, was queasy and refused to touch a bite of the sandwich and glass of red wine he was offered.

And that night, in the midst of the meal around four A.M., there was even entertainment: a woman, a tramp from somewhere—perhaps she had been a music hall singer once—gave us an outrageous recital of popular songs.

THE URINALS OF PARIS

OTHER cities modestly hid their public urinals below the ground. Paris, like the good Latin city it is, erected them out in the open, in public squares, on the streets. In the thirties, there were more than 1,300 of them. These miniature shelters in various styles—round or square, graceful, clumsy, sometimes baroque, topped off with one or more lamps—often resembled sentry boxes or advertising kiosks, even pagodas. Their genealogy goes back to the first century of our era, to the days of the Emperor Vespasian, the first benefactor to offer amphoras to the Romans for use as urinals.

Most of the **pissotières** in Paris date from around 1900. There has been great argument as to their aesthetic value, and even their utility. Are they not exclusively and selfishly reserved for the use of men? But like the Morris Columns and the Wallace Fountains, like the newspaper kiosks, they have become familiar sights in the Parisian urban landscape. Henry Miller spoke of them frequently, with tears in his eyes. He praised the French for having almost always known just how to pick the best spot on which to erect one. He gives lyrical descriptions of these places, "where the water gurgles melodiously." "There are," he wrote, "some urinals that I go out of my way to visit, like the old, dilapidated one in front of the school for deaf-mutes on the corner of the Rue Saint-Jacques and the Rue Abbé-de-l'Epée."

At nightfall, the urinal lamps lit up with the streetlamps. These tiny chapels served an odd religion. They were public conveniences, but also meeting grounds and cruising areas for homosexuals, particularly the round urinals with three stalls, whose circular layout allowed for direct contact. Darkness was also part of the attraction. "Darkness," Proust wrote, "has the effect of eliminating the first stage of pleasure and of allowing us to enter straightaway into a world of caresses at which we usually arrive only after some time has passed. . . . In the darkness, all of the old habits fall away, hands, lips, bodies can act immediately." And Proust mentions this "immediate response of the body which does not withdraw, which approaches [and] gives us an unprejudiced notion of the person we silently address, full of vice, a notion that provides us the additional pleasure of having succeeded in tasting the fruit without having desired it with our eyes, and without having asked permission." In those days, this somber ballet, the comings and goings of the inverts, went on throughout the night. Neither the smell nor the dirt of these places repulsed the devotees of Greek love. On the contrary. The more malodorous the chapels, the more popular they became.

The vice squad would turn up occasionally, and many famous names in the arts and literature, or in high society, fell into its net. Proust, who was the first to dare reveal in his novel the underside of Sodom and Gomorrah—with more irony than charity—did not leave out the **vespasiennes**. Of course, the Baron de Charlus was an assiduous visitor. "The Baron de Charlus must have caught a disease," the Duc de Guermantes's valet naïvely tells him, "to stand about as long as he does in the **pistière**. I saw him go into the **pistière** in the Rue de Bourgogne. When I came back from Neuilly over an hour later, I saw his yellow trousers, in the same **pistière**, in the same place, in the middle stall where he always goes so that people shan't see him" **(The Captive)**. Considered an outrage to public decency, such a misdemeanor could cost as much as from two months to three years in prison and a fine of from 500 to 4,500 francs. Despite this risk, despite the sentence, the inverts faithfully patronized their tearooms, their "cups," as the urinals were called, and the nocturnal ballet continued with renewed vigor.

To put a stop to such practices, the Paris Municipal Council moved a few years back to get rid of all of them, and they began with the tearooms with three communicating stalls. So the habitués, on a certain evening, would walk up and find nothing but an empty spot where their favorite chapel had once stood. From 1,300 the number of **pissotières** fell gradually to 350, and soon they will all be gone. Having become historical monuments, like the art nouveau subway entrances that are already being collected, will they be installed in museums and in collections in the New World? And won't France be sorry one day to have taken so little care to preserve them? "For," as Henry Miller wrote, "how can a Frenchman know that one of the first things that strikes the eye of a newly arrived American, and which moves him and warms his guts, is this omnipresent urinal?"

THE UNDERWORLD
THE POLICE

THERE are many similarities between what we call the "underworld" and the "fashionable world." Entry into both these exclusive societies, made up primarily of the idle, is not easy. Each has its regulations, its customs and usages, its moral code, its affairs of honor, whether its members settle them with sabers, pistols, or knives. If entry into "high society" requires family crests, titles, diplomas from the best schools, wealth and fame, entry into the underworld requires widespread criminal activity, a police record full of arrests, and, of course, an illegitimate background, suspicious forebears, closely supervised training. Even the languages are similar, both tainted with snobbery. Just as the polished speech of men of the world is, at least in France, full of Anglicisms and fashionable catch phrases, so criminal slang, continually changing, is full of words newly coined from the streets of Paris. I even noticed that in the underworld some of the guys, out of pure snobbery, spoke a slang so hermetic that even their pals couldn't understand them. They had to translate their ideas into French to make themselves understood. Isn't this kind of snobbery contrary to the very spirit and purpose of slang, which is to protect people, to create solidarity among a similar class? Yet paradoxically, snobbery forms the basis of slang. Slang—trivial, obscene, but so poetic, all images, metaphors—is in constant danger of losing its expressive force. Thus it is forever inventing new phrases, discarding many words as outdated, outmoded. There is a plethora of synonyms for every kind of person, idea, or thing that touches the underworld. I've counted some of them: twenty expressions for the verb "to love," some thirty for "to kiss," a dozen for sexual arousal, the same number for ejaculation, more than seventy words—a record!—for the act of love. There are fifty words for the male sex organ, fifteen for the testicles, twenty or so for the female organ, twenty words for breasts, twenty for the buttocks. There are more than sixty different expressions for prostitution, thirty for pimp, twenty for whorehouse, a dozen for madam, forty for male homosexual, six for lesbian. And in the area of crime and violence, there are thirty words for police, ten for informer, ten for prison. As for "escape," "flight," "arrest," and "prison," for each of these, thirty different words. There's another strange thing about slang: Parisian argot has given pimps the names of fish: mackerel, mac, mec, herring, wrasse or peacock fish, pike, mullet, barbel, or simply "fish" . . . So, with its usual wit, argot's term for the fountain in the Place Pigalle around which the mackerels stand guard over their protégées while they work is the "aquarium." Another curious thing is that in argot the police are given the names of birds: the police are "fowl," policemen are "chickens," criminal investigators are "partridges," prison is the "hen-house," the "coop," and policemen on bicycles are "swallows." This latter term is the only true metaphor: with their flowing black capes, these policemen seem to have swallows' wings and they sweep as silently through the streets, around corners, brushing against the walls, as do these lively and graceful birds. In slang, they are also known as **"cyclos,"** "pilgrims" (because of the capes), and "pigs on wheels."

Most of the pimps in Paris used to be Corsican or North African. There were some Arabs or Kabyles, arriving in town almost illiterate, beginning as simple laborers, street vendors, or stevedores at Les Halles, who rapidly become small-time and then big-time "chiefs," with a "stable" of two or three women to wear out their high heels for them on the sidewalks. Their favorite neighborhood was the Goutte d'Or, in the XVIIIth arrondissement, which was a North Africa in miniature. Its bars and cafés played only Arab music, and in some of them there were half-naked women doing the belly dance. Then some of the Arab chiefs moved in their Cadillacs to strongholds in the Place Pigalle and the Place Blanche, where the business of love had hitherto been controlled by the Corsican underworld. And then it was war; there were bloody gang killings worthy of Chicago. For many years the front pages of the newspapers were full of these shootouts, these settlings of scores, with their many dead.

Up to the beginning of the nineteenth century, dangerous criminals were called **malandrins,** or "brigands." Then they were called "bandits." It was only at the beginning of the twentieth century that they were given the name "apaches." This name came into vogue during the "Casque d'Or" affair, in 1902. Two gangs led by rival pimps in Charonne confronted each other in a bloody free-for-all over a seductive lady of easy virtue known as Casque d'Or, for her flaming hair. A newspaperman then gave one of these gangs the name "apaches," after the Texas Indian tribe. The name rapidly spread, and for twenty some years, all criminals were known as **apaches.** Only after the First World War was **apache** superseded by **gangster,** also trans-Atlantic, and up until now, nothing has taken the place of **gangsterism** and **gangs**—even the police have become an **anti-gang.** And their job has grown increasingly difficult. So long as prostitutes were registered and in houses, the police were easily able to keep tabs on the underworld. They often worked closely with the girls. Likewise, the dance halls, night clubs, and bars frequented exclusively by hoods were like open sores the police had been able to isolate, if not cure. Given a few well-placed informers, the authors of past or future crimes could be picked up easily enough. Members of the underworld, proud of

showing off, also set themselves apart by their dress. An extra-flat cap worn down over the eyes was as necessary for them as a society gentleman's polished top hat.

The underworld is not dead. Indeed, it's more alive than ever, but its traditional surroundings did not survive the War and the Occupation. Its meeting places, its way of life, have changed profoundly. The armed attacks, the nocturnal jewel heists, the bank robberies, holdups, drug operations, all these are now planned in elegant neighborhoods by men who shop at the best stores. So, since 1964 the criminal police have been forced to establish an **anti-gang** brigade whose real job is not to catch criminals, but to forestall the crime itself, by keeping a tight surveillance over criminal activities. An army of stool pigeons and microphones listens in barbershops, in expensive restaurants, in night clubs and fashionable cafés, for nowadays, the underworld is part and parcel of high society.

The Escaped Con

Late one night, Rue Quincampoix. I was photographing the girls as they plied their trade in front of the one-night hotels. I had only taken a couple of pictures when, as though at some mysterious password, their "protectors" came running from all sides. They were going to smash my camera and rough me up . . . We would have to make a quick getaway. Along with Robert, my young assistant, I ran as fast as I could toward the safety of the lights on the Boulevard Sébastopol. A huge fellow, more determined than the others, continued to come after us. We ran all the way to the outskirts of Les Halles.

"Don't be scared, pal," our pursuer called out, panting. "I don't want to hurt you. Stop . . ."

I stopped, but I didn't feel any too safe. What if this was a trick and he stabbed me with his switchblade?

"Don't be afraid of those bums. I'm the man you want. I'll keep them quiet," he gasped.

I understood he was offering to protect us from the underworld. "I've got a tight asshole, pal, made of iron; you can count on me. I know how to get around

those guys. I'm not a pimp, it's just a put-on. I'm an escaped con . . . So I've got girls coming out my ass, see?"

Still wary, I searched his face. He thumped his chest. "I'm not kidding. Look, I'll show you . . ."

He took off his jacket, then his shirt. Naked to the waist, he motioned me over beneath a streetlight. "Take a look. I'm telling you the truth . . ."

His torso was like a wall covered with graffiti: hearts, sirens, dragons, a skull, a huge naked woman on his stomach who moved when he breathed. A masterpiece of tattooing. Each picture had a story behind it, marking some adventure, escape, a love affair, even perhaps a murder. His body was the diary of his life.

"I'm mucked up from head to foot," he said, pleased by my admiration. And he invited me to visit him the next evening somewhere in Belleville, where he was holed up. He scribbled his address for me on a scrap of paper.

"I'm laying low there and I'll wait for you. But remember, pal, mum's the word. Don't squeal on me."

I certainly didn't lack the desire to see him again . . . but we didn't speak the same language: I was really scared he might carve me up, rub me out . . .

LOVERS

Unlike other cities, other countries, Paris has always been indulgent toward lovers. Even kissing on the mouth in public has never been forbidden. There have always been alleyways full of tenderly embracing couples after a dance or the movies. Couples kiss on public benches, in the subway, under streetlights, and nobody is shocked, no one pays any attention. The girl usually stands with her back against a wall, against a hoarding or a doorway, as though her escort wanted to protect her. The waiting rooms in railway stations, public squares, the Jardins du Luxembourg and the Jardins des Tuileries, are always classic meeting places for lovers.

THE BALS-MUSETTE

THE ancestors of the popular dance hall were the lower-class public dance halls—**bals-musette**—and rustic pleasure gardens on the outskirts of Paris. There one went to dance to the nasal sound of a wind instrument related to the Breton pipes or the Scotch bagpipe, called the **musette**. As Paris gradually expanded outside its walls and absorbed its surrounding suburbs and villages, many of these rural cabarets were also absorbed into the city itself. And the **musette** was gradually dethroned by the tremulous sound of the accordion.

Not until the Belle Epoque, however, do we find an increase in the number of these popular dance halls, with their picturesque names, frequented by **apaches** and their girls: La Chemise Sale ("The Dirty Shirt"), Le Progrès, La Tête de Cochon, and so on. It is a mystery how the Rue de Lappe, a sordid street near Les Halles, became the favorite street for pimps, but it was there that the ladies of easy virtue and their young hoods began to congregate. Even the regular employees of established whorehouses came there on their days off. And one after the other, in red lights the color of blood, the signs of a dozen popular dance halls went up, giving an air of tragedy to this ill-famed street: Le Bal des Quatre Saisons, Le Petit Balcon, La Musette, La Bal des Familles,

La Boule Rouge. There was another cluster of low-life dance halls around the Arts et Métiers building, near the Boulevard Sébastopol, particularly in the sarcastically named Rue des Vertus, whose reputation dates back to the sixteenth century. Each dance hall had its special clientele: on the Rue de Valence, the "gangs" of the period; at the Bal de la Montagne Sainte-Geneviève, homosexuals; at the dance hall in the Rue Fagon, near the Place d'Italie, Arab pimps; at the Bal de la Marine on the Quai de Grenelle and Au Clair de Lune in the Place d'Italie, sailors and servant girls.

Most of these dance halls still had shady reputations in the thirties. There were no "Paris by Night" buses unloading tourists avid to rub elbows with the underworld. No cosmopolitan breeze blew through these typically Parisian oases. The dance hall had **its** fashion, **its** music, **its** code, and also its typical, unvarying decor: red imitation-leather banquettes, tables solidly nailed to the floor—against possible fights—large mirrors, lamps with Venetian-glass globes, multicolored paper streamers festooned from the four corners of the ceiling to the center of the room, where a prismed, multifaceted ball was hung, casting confetti of light over the walls and the dancing couples, wafting them into a starry sky. The dance halls were full of poetry and dreams, but they were also full of pitfalls: true love came close to prostitution. In these dance halls, young pimps seduced girls and recruited the labor force for the streets and the whorehouses.

The dance hall also had its fashion in dress, and this was the real folk costume of Paris. The girls wore skirts with suspenders, satin blouses, and those spit-curls—or kiss-curls—which were so typical: small coiled locks of hair flattened onto the forehead or the temples. As for the guys, they all wore caps which nothing in the world could have made them remove. Only the band was allowed some latitude for fantasy. It was usually composed of musicians from Auvergne dressed up as Brazilian Cariocas or Argentine gauchos, and every band had its accordion player who was the "One and Only," its "World-Famous" singer who would croon languorous tangos, rowdy waltzes, and the latest java into a megaphone. Need I say that the immodest, provocative, and vulgar sound of the java was, at least before the last war, the only typically French popular music, the only living, animated music that originated in the Parisian dance halls.

Some of the customers would sit at tables; others would stand around the

bar, where the drinks were half-price. Their caps either pulled down over their eyes or pushed back from their foreheads, they would sip colored drinks—green, red, violet, orange—through straws. Because of the constant threat of brawls, it was forbidden to serve drinks by the bottle—that would have furnished dangerous ammunition.

An invitation to dance was made at long distance. In places like this, no man got up and bowed to a woman. He gave her a hard stare from across the room and emitted a loud, sonorous psst! The sounds—Psst! Psst!—shot from table to table in every direction before every dance, like an orchestra of crickets! Yet, no sooner would these couples take a few turns on the floor, bouncing around, the men's hands around the small of the girls' backs, than the band would grind to a halt and the owner's voice would ring forth: "Shell out! Shell out!" And each dancer would dig into his pocket and pull out twenty-five centimes, five sous, the price per dance. Only the men paid. And the band would strike up again.

According to the strict etiquette that prevailed, no woman had the right to turn down a stranger's invitation to dance, even if she was with an escort, even if she was new to the place. Also, a girl who accepted an invitation to have a drink with one of the regulars was tacitly agreeing to go to bed with him. A refusal could cause a brawl. Other pretexts for a fight were: a mistress's infidelity or betrayal or a girl's changing neighborhoods to escape from her pimp. These brawls, these "settlings of account," usually didn't occur inside the dance hall, but in the street outside, after closing time. A dreadful and dreaded moment! Knives flashed from pockets, and out of the women's corsets and garters. There were real pitched battles between rival gangs, between the clients of different dance halls or from different neighborhoods. So that the police wouldn't interfere, some dance halls were located at the ends of private alleys, where cops had no right to go.

The public dance halls gradually lost their bad reputation. Tradition was overturned by a man known as Jo de France. He got the idea of turning these small dance halls into something gigantic, spectacular. He leased a huge ballroom on the Rue de Lappe and there he re-created the atmosphere of the French films of the thirties, like **Sous les Toits de Paris**, with decorations reminiscent of unsavory streets, lampposts and whorehouses, houses with peeling façades, all under a starry sky. With the opening of the Balajo—Jo's

Dance Hall—the street of the popular dance halls was turned over to tourist buses, to foreign visitors eager to spend a night on the town and rub elbows with the underworld. And the French too, out of curiosity, a yen for low-life, were drawn to the Rue de Lappe, even the bourgeois from Passy and the aristocrats from the Faubourg Saint-Germain. A member of the aristocracy went so far as to buy one of these dance halls in order to offer his elegant friends the thrill of shaking a leg alongside the lower classes in their caps. Among the Parisian aristocracy, Proust remarks, there were many who, like the Baron de Charlus, enjoyed themselves only with the lower classes. "The Baron now passed his life entirely among social inferiors, thus, without knowing it, continuing the tradition of not a few of his illustrious ancestors, the Duc de La Rochefoucauld, the Prince d'Harcourt, the Duc de Berry, whom Saint-Simon pictures to us as spending their lives among their lackeys—to such a point that it was embarrassing" (**The Past Recaptured**).

As for the younger generation, they have since the War begun to be bored by the "old-fashioned" décor of these dance halls, by the accordion orchestras and the jerky waltzes. They have turned to jazz, to jukeboxes, to rock. The underworld has changed, too. The menacing atmosphere of former days hasn't disappeared, far from it, but the underworld has abandoned its former ways of life, its habitual, clearly defined fiefdoms, which were too accessible to the police. Now, the mobsters prefer the bars along the Champs-Elysées to the saloons and dives of the Rue de Lappe. The red neon signs still wink at the passers-by, but they are no longer menacing. Nothing is left of the dance halls of yesterday but their décor, their picturesque and anachronistic customers, and the accordion, which still holds forth beneath the starry sky.

LA MÔME BIJOU

ONE winter night in 1932, around two in the morning, I went into a small bar in Montmartre, the Bar de la Lune. The first figure I made out through the cloud of smoke was that of an ageless woman who was sitting alone with a glass of red wine in her hand. Her dark clothes glittered strangely. Her bosom was covered with an incredible quantity of jewelry: brooches, lavaliers, chokers, clips, chains—a veritable Christmas tree of garlands, of glittering stars.

And rings! She wore more than a dozen—two on each plump finger, crammed on up to her knuckles, which were entwined in the fake pearls of the necklaces she had wrapped like bracelets around her wrists.

I was struck by this fantastic apparition that had sprung up out of the night, like an entomologist by a rare and monstrously beautiful insect. I had discovered what had to be the queen of Montmartre's nocturnal fauna.

"You don't know her?" the bartender asked me, surprised at my astonishment. "It's La Môme Bijou—Miss Diamonds. Once she was rich and famous, led the good life. When people still had carriages, she rode in the Bois de Boulogne in her barouche . . . Now she lives on charity, she reads the customers' palms . . ."

Fascinated, I devoured her with my eyes. Miss Diamonds was a palette

come to life, refined. The dark mass of her old-fashioned black velvet cape, ragged and torn, shiny in spots, topped off with a moth-eaten fur collar, her black evening dress in the style of 1900, all silk and lace, brought out the greens, purples, pale pinks, the nacreous colors of fake pearls, the glitter of paste jewelry, of fake rubies, fake turquoises, fake emeralds. The palette of Gustave Moreau . . . Her face, with its white clown make-up, was softened by a green veil decorated with roses.

And yet—behind her glittering eyes, still seductive, lit with the lights of the Belle Epoque, as if they had escaped the onslaughts of age, the ghost of a pretty girl seemed to smile out. Had Miss Diamonds really been a **demi-mondaine**, a younger sister to Cléo de Mérode, Liane de Pougy, La Belle Otero, Odette de Crécy—all dear to the heart of Marcel Proust—or had she walked the streets from the Moulin Rouge to the Place Pigalle, going from bar to bar, from one dance hall to another, one body to another, as some of the patrons of the bar told me? I wanted to know about her life, to have her tell me her memories. Where did she live? Did she sleep in a four-poster bed hung with veils and lace, or did she sleep on a pile of rags? Would she show me her old photographs, the proofs of her gilded past? It was too late to strike up a conversation with her. I took only three photographs, but I intended to return another evening. Alas, I never saw Miss Diamonds again.

One morning, after my **Paris de Nuit** had come out in 1933, Miss Diamonds put in an unforgettable appearance at my publisher's office. Swathed in her tawdry finery, outrageously made up, she created a panic. Removed from her surroundings, deprived of the night's complicity, revealed in the light of day, she was monstrous. "You published my picture in your book," she shouted threateningly. "You printed nasty things about me. Do I seem to be 'escaped out of a nightmare of Baudelaire'? Do I? Me, a nightmare? You'll pay for it!" And she refused to leave until the publisher had paid her for the "insult."

Jean Giraudoux's **The Madwoman of Chaillot**, written in 1943 during the Occupation and first performed on December 21, 1945, at the Athénée, dragged Miss Diamonds out of the shadows. At the time, she was thought to have been the inspiration for Giraudoux's play. And since it was also performed in London and New York, she became world famous. "I remember her well," Joseph Kessel wrote on the day following the premiere. "You used to see her at dawn in Montmartre, when the night gave rise to fatigue and hallucinations. She would suddenly turn up in some **brasserie** on the Boulevard de Clichy or in a delicatessen on the Place Pigalle, and no one would pay much attention. They were used to her, she was one of the night people, one of the troubled. Men in the bars would buy her sausages and red wine to get her to tell her stories. Every morning she was drunk, and she never laughed. A horrible, fascinating old woman, on the brink of madness, on the brink of decay, she had an indefinable air of grace, of love . . ."

Miss Diamonds wasn't the only model Giraudoux had. There was another madwoman, the Madwoman of Alma. And the play's heroine, Aurélia, was a mixture of these two eccentrics. Unlike Miss Diamonds, the Madwoman of Alma was an extremely rich woman, and not an ex-courtesan. She could sometimes be glimpsed around the Place d'Alma, laden with baubles, necklaces, semiprecious stones, feathers, bows, and velvet ribbons, with a scarf of Valenciennes lace around her neck, her head wrapped in a cloud of tulle. Indifferent to the passers-by, she would stroll along majestically under her lace parasol like a sleepwalker. If Miss Diamonds is better known than the Madwoman of Alma, it is because of my photographs, which were used in designing the play's costumes, whereas no picture exists, that I am aware, of the Madwoman of Alma.

Thirty years later, in 1963 at the Menton Palais du Louvre, we were hanging the photographs in my show which had been exhibited earlier at the Bibliothèque Nationale; I had included my photograph of Miss Diamonds, and it had appeared that morning in a Nice newspaper. Suddenly, an old man, still vigorous and neatly dressed, came into the Palais and asked to see me. "Sir, are you the author of this photograph? When I opened my paper, I got quite a shock. So you knew her! I wanted to know, because in my younger days, I was Miss Diamonds' lover . . ."

A miraculous encounter. Would I finally learn the true story of Miss

Diamonds? "It was a long time ago," my visitor told me. "I could tell you so many things . . ."

Unfortunately, the installation was not finished, and I excused myself, promising the noble old man that I was immensely interested in his story and that I would visit him in a few days. Visibly disappointed—he was trembling with eagerness—he presented me with his card and left.

I kept my word. But when I got to his hotel, one of those old, dilapidated Menton palaces dating from the time of the Grand Dukes, and mentioned his name—Dumont-Charterêt—I was met with dismay at the desk. Delays, consultations, telephone calls. After a long wait, the concierge asked me, "Are you a member of the family?"

"No," I said, "but Monsieur Dumont-Charterêt wants to see me. We made an appointment on the telephone. Would you please announce me?"

"I'm sorry, sir, but that's impossible . . ."

"Impossible? Why?"

"Monsieur Dumont-Charterêt has just died. He died suddenly yesterday afternoon. I'm sorry, sir."

My aged gallant carried his secret with him to his grave. And so I will never know the true story of Miss Diamonds.

LADIES OF THE EVENING

Paris has never had a red-light district **per se**, where the girls, seated in windows overlooking the street, could display their wares to passers-by. But there have always been **quartiers chauds**—"hot spots"—in Paris. It would be boring to name them all.

Myself, I preferred the district around Les Halles. Famous for its central market—known as the Belly of Paris—the area also dealt in the lower parts of the body. Of course, people went there to sniff the odors of vegetables, fruits, flowers, and cheese, but they also went for the sight of the motley crowds of women standing in doorways—often quite attractive women—dressed (and undressed) in strange costumes. The girls would congregate in bunches on the steps of the small one-night hotels. At dawn, a day shift would take over from the night shift. From four in the morning on, these Venuses of the Crossroads were at their posts, offering their charms to the stevedores and farmers, and to the night people who had spent the evening in Montmartre or in Montparnasse and were now capping it off at Les Halles. Throughout the quarter, around the ancient church of Saint-Merri, one could smell the fumes of venal love: the stones, the pavements, the very walls had been impregnated with it for eight or nine centuries. Perhaps it was no fluke that an Italian kid named Giovanni Boccaccio, who grew up to become the author of one of the most risqué books ever written, the **Decameron,** was born here in 1313, on the Rue des Lombards, which is to this day a street famous for its whores. It forms an angle with the decaying Rue Quincampoix. During the seventeenth century, before becoming a depot for packing cases and crates belonging to the merchants of Les Halles, and a den of Arabs, this street was the head-quarters of the bank owned by the financier Law until his notorious bank-ruptcy. In the thirties, the Rue Quincampoix had another specialty: it was full of fat girls, "floozies," who were called **"Nanas," "punaises," "morues"** ("bed-bugs" and "codfish") in slang. Contrary to the mobility streetwalkers usually display, they waited, immobile and placid, along the sidewalk like a row of caryatids for the butchers and tripe-sellers from Les Halles, men who were accustomed to dealing with huge masses of flesh. One day I took a room in a hotel across the street and watched from my window these odalisques and the men who would stroll past them ten or more times, back and forth, cigarettes dangling from their lips, before stopping in front of their choice. The hotel I was in was not a bordello, but what was known as a "hump house." The girls nevertheless had a close relationship with the owner, just as if they were his boarders. Rival hotels would offer all kinds of extra services to get their patronage. In the one I was in, the owner not only paid the girls a percentage of the room rent he charged them per customer, but also offered a kind of insurance for sick leave, pregnancy, or imprisonment. He even undertook to send monthly maintenance checks to his "boarders'" children. Most of them were very affectionate mothers. Their life stories had been the same for centuries: unknown father, bastard child. "Nearly all of them had in the background faithless men, broken promises, joy paid for by poverty," wrote Balzac in **La Peau de Chagrin.** They had known nothing of maternal or paternal affection; thus the power their "protectors" had over them. They preferred being exploited, even brutalized, to enduring solitude. Although they were not ashamed to make their living by their bodies—some were even proud of it—they could not be said to have been really happy. They all lived on

hope. Every one of them dreamed of a different, a better life. Their dreams were all the same: to earn enough money to open a little business as soon as they could, to make a good marriage, to be called "Mrs.," but money ran through their fingers. They were big spenders, they smoked, drank, even took drugs. Few of them had the will-power to save money. And once they had a police record, it was difficult to get rid of the stigma. Up until 1946, any woman caught soliciting three times, or picked up in a raid on a cheap hotel with a man whose name she didn't know, got a record at the Prefecture of Police. This record was a millstone around her neck for the rest of her life.

Beneath their surface gaiety, these girls lived in perpetual anxiety. They were fearful of raids, of the Black Maria, the police station, prison. They were afraid of becoming sick. They were afraid of every stranger. What if he turned out to be a sadist, kinky, a dangerous maniac, a Jack the Ripper? They also lived in fear of their "protector," of his whims and bad moods. Like some modern suzerain, he could put his protégé in a brothel, sell her to a colleague, send her abroad. And beware to any girl who ran away or talked back. There were violent scenes, penalties were exacted, even death. The long pitiless arm of the underworld would follow her and find her wherever she went.

While on the street, the girls were obsessed by the "chickens," the "partridges," the members of the vice squad. Some girls could smell their approach. "I smell cops." "They're on the way!" The alert given, the street would empty of girls as if by magic. They had a strange mixture of solidarity and rivalry. United against the vice squad, they were still ready to fight to protect the place they had struggled so hard to get: a section of sidewalk, a corner. Any colleague who tried to take over their turf had better watch out. At such times, they would often call on their protectors for help. On the other hand, when it came to helping a sister who had fallen on hard times, their solidarity would emerge. A girl who worked the Place Blanche had been hit by a car and had had to have both her legs amputated. Her colleagues in the neighborhood arranged to have her carried out every day to the café from which she had plied her trade before her accident. Thus, at secondhand, she was able to continue to partake in their life. And after each trick, all the girls would discreetly slip a bill into a money box under her table.

My hotel was more comfortable than its sordid façade and leprous walls

indicated. Each room had heavy, flowered curtains, a wardrobe with mirror, a large all-purpose bed, and looked as though it had been decorated by the Douanier Rousseau. There was also a rug and that most important piece of furniture, a bidet. Down in the hall below, the patroness distributed towels and kept track of the tricks. Some girls never went downstairs. They waited patiently in their rooms for their regular clients—their subscribers, rather—to arrive. During the rush hour, around ten in the evening, some of them would just throw coats over their naked bodies and go down to the street in their carpet slippers, eager not to waste any time. One of their great concerns: where to hide the "take," the money they earned from their tricks? Handbags? Too vulnerable. Some girls hid a small purse in some intimate part of their bodies, stuck between their buttocks or onto their upper thighs with adhesive tape. Others hid the big bills carefully folded in their flowered garters, in their garter belts, in the lining of their skirts, or down between their breasts.

One day in this hotel I witnessed a strange scene. A tall blond girl appeared, and her sisters dashed up to her, kissed her: "It's Eliane, Eliane's back, she's come back from Saint-Lago!" The good news spread through the establishment, and there were shrieks of joy. Eliane had missed two medical visits and had therefore been carted off for a few days' confinement in Saint-Lazare. Although prostitutes in whorehouses were visited by the doctor "at home," streetwalkers were required to report once a week to a dispensary in the Prefecture of Police to put their feet in the stirrups—"mount the camel," as the examination position was known in slang.

In 1932, the year I took my pictures in the Rue Quincampoix, Saint-Lazare was still a going concern. Since the Terror during the French Revolution, this sordid building had been the place where prostitutes were interned. It wasn't closed until 1935, when its role as a women's prison was taken over by La Roquette. At one time, prostitutes were put behind bars for minor infractions: they were forbidden to begin work until a half-hour after the streetlights were lit, or before seven P.M. in the summertime. They had to wear a white bonnet and apron to distinguish them from respectable women. They were forbidden to appear on main thoroughfares; to be seen on the Rue de Rivoli or in the Tuileries cost them eight days in prison—two weeks for the Grands Boulevards. I also had a strange encounter in this hotel. I thought I recognized the face of a girl who was wearing a black leather mini-skirt. She looked like a girl I had run into once on the Boulevard de la Madeleine, all dolled up then and wearing a fake mink. The change was so striking that I didn't think it could be the same person—but it was. And she explained the reasons for her transformation from high-class call girl to common whore. Even though the price for a trick had been ten times higher at the Madeleine than it was here, she had earned less. She had done less business and her expenses—daily hair-set, manicure, laundry, clothes, drinks—had been enormous.

The abolition of prostitute registration by the police naturally didn't wipe out prostitution. And the closing of the bordellos in 1946, sending thousands of girls onto the streets, also led to an increase in their number, estimated to have been around a half-million at the time. The character of prostitution, however, has changed enormously. The sexual revolution took away the younger clientele. Today, in the Quartier Latin, for example, there are practically no prostitutes at all. And the streetwalkers who are still working the sidewalks attract only the old, the ugly, the solitary, foreigners, perverts. In place of a trade whose charm was perhaps too visible, too provocative, there has gradually grown up a hidden, but nonetheless flourishing, prostitution. And more often than not in the better neighborhoods. Today the girls prefer to hang out in bars or cafés, where they are backed by the owners, the waiters, or the doormen and desk clerks in the larger hotels. Some of them work out of their homes, or in places where they are tolerated by the police. Nowadays, their main tools are the telephone, the address book, the automobile, and nude photographs of themselves in seductive poses.

BERGER
CINZANO
LE MEILLEUR APERITIF
HOTEL
DE
NANTES
CONFORT MODERNE
HOTEL

"HOUSES OF ILLUSION"

Like streetwalkers, they were shrouded in mystery. Their eternally closed shutters, their red lights, their huge numbers lit up late into the night, set them apart from the neighboring bourgeois houses. Some had no name, but only a gigantic number in the style of the period, art nouveau, cubist, art deco: Number 9, Number 26, Number 43, Number 122, Number 162, were all famous. Sometimes they had multicolored windows, picturesque façades or entrances, like the Japonaise near the Porte Saint-Denis, or the Suzy in the Rue Grégoire-de-Tours. There were many names for them, but they all meant brothel: **maison close, maison de tolérance, maison publique, maison d'illusions,** or simply **maison** ("house"), and in slang there were many more: **bordel, boxon, bobinard, magasin de fesses** . . .

In the thirties, these houses still represented a lucrative and flourishing industry. On the one hand, there was the brothel trade itself. The houses were owned by respectable families and institutions, as well as by the underworld—retired mobsters, mostly Corsicans. On the other hand, there was the recruitment and placement of the girls. Each house had its official "whole-

 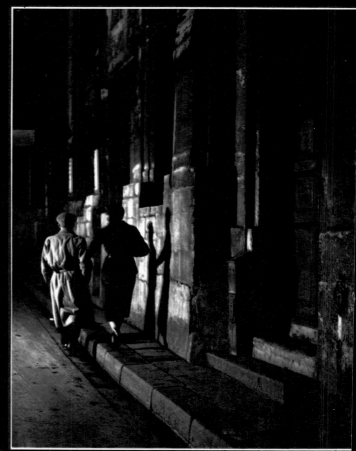

saler"—its purveyor or, in slang reminiscent of the butcher shop, its "meat man." Several hundred purveyors brought home the bacon for the 800 bordellos of France. They went off on buying trips, delivered the "goods" to earn their tips—"posies" or "bouquets" as they were called then—from the brothel owners. The recruiters had to be handsome and, above all, have a good line in order to seduce the naïve or desperate girls who came to Paris to make their fortunes; they had to be seductive. These young mobsters picked the girls up as they arrived at the station, got friendly with them, and delivered them—after a few days of tender lovemaking—to an experienced older hand, a "pro," who would train them for the profession. Other good hunting grounds for these pimps were street fairs and dance halls.

Every quarter of Paris had its brothels, large and small, supervised by the City Hall and the municipal government. The VIth arrondissement, which includes Montparnasse, Saint-Germain-des-Prés, the Quartier Latin, was proud of having the greatest number. There were five on the Rue Mazarine alone. Some girls lived upstairs in the house, in dormitory cubicles, as they were called. Others went home once their work was finished. If they lived with a "protector," they were required to hand over their take, the money they earned from their tricks. Despite the rather modest standing of the smaller houses, the girls made a good living. Their daily earnings depended as much on the number of their tricks as on the price they charged. The girls didn't lie around doing nothing in these smaller houses. The atmosphere was also more friendly and less affected there, more free and easy, the talk less formal.

The more sumptuous of these houses were located in the heart of Paris, around the Opéra and the Palais Royal. In the thirties, the Colbert, 4 Rue de Hanovre, the Saint-Augustin, the Château d'Eau, were still flourishing. It was in a bordello in the tiny Rue des Moulins, which comes out onto the Avenue de l'Opéra, that Toulouse-Lautrec painted his idle **pensionnaires** awaiting their clients in the salon. Another bordello, in the Rue des Martyrs, acquired a rather scandalous reputation when the elderly president of the French senate died there one night in a girl's arms. The One-Two-Two, at Number 122 Rue de Provence, opened well before the First World War, was one of the favorite houses of the upper classes. Number 14, the Montyon, on the same street, near the Grands Boulevards, was frequented by Degas. In his famous monotype illustrations for Maupassant's **La Maison Tellier**, Degas was inspired by the girls and the madam of that luxurious house. Picasso showed me eleven of them; they were the gems of his collection. His favorite was one entitled **Madam's Birthday**, in which all the girls in the establishment, stark naked except for black stockings, are crowding around the patroness, teasing her. As evidence of his admiration for Degas, Picasso introduced his profile into many of his own erotic engravings. Founded by a former valet to Louis-Philippe, richly decorated with paintings, sculptures, tapestries, and mirrors, the Montyon was the outstanding Parisian house during the Second Empire, and unique of its kind. Many members of the nobility frequented its "House of Lords," which was world famous. Around 1900, the Montyon was superseded by a new house, the most luxurious in the world. This, the most famous of Parisian brothels, was built on the site of the Hotel Chabanais Saint-Ponges, and it soon became the center of elegant life, a national institution, a kind of League of Nations. It was a place which the great names of society, high finance, diplomacy, and even crowned heads made sure to include in the official program of their visits, and where they met. The obese and jovial Edward VII, to console himself during his endless years as Prince of Wales—Victoria reigned sixty-four years and did not decide to die until she was eighty-two—had a "Hindu Room" set up in the Chabanais in homage to his mother, the Empress of India. A sumptuous four-poster bore his crest, not to mention the extraordinary bathtub of red copper, adorned with caryatids, which the Prince of Wales sometimes ordered to be filled with champagne in which to immerse his chosen one. There was a curious armchair with three seats known as "The Indiscreet," especially designed for His Royal Highness, which enabled him to amuse himself with two women simultaneously. The intimate Franco-English relationships established at the Chabanais must have been of great help in concluding the Entente Cordiale.

Since the Chabanais was to be a showcase of French taste and elegance, an army of artisans, artists, and decorators—and even ethnographers and archeologists—labored to give it a luxury unparalleled at the time. No bordello had ever had such a wealth of chandeliers, tapestries, Venetian mirrors, rooms with "themes"—very much in vogue—of such elegance: Moorish rooms, Pompeian rooms, the Chinese Pagoda, all with appropriate music and cos-

tumes, struck visitors with astonishment and admiration. There was the Louis XVI boudoir, in homage to Marie Antoinette, and the Louis XV boudoir, for Madame de Pompadour. There was also the inevitable torture chamber, with all its accessories: handcuffs, whips, hunting crops, flails. The Japanese Room was given an official prize at the 1900 World's Fair as an example of French refinement and taste.

In these large upper-class "houses of illusion," the staff was never completely undressed. Naked bodies were covered with sumptuous negligees. These were like transparent evening dresses, with silk trains, decorated with bows, covered with lace. They were cut low to reveal bare arms and bosoms. Around 1900, prices in these houses ranged from ten to forty francs. At the Chabanais, the price of a trick, drinks and tip included, was at least fifty francs. At the Moulins—frequented by Toulouse-Lautrec—you could get away with twenty francs. The price was high, however, when you consider that in an ordinary whorehouse it was only two francs. In principle, the staff received half the fee. In reality, the house took a good deal more by providing food, clothing, hairdressers, make-up, laundry, et cetera, at exorbitant prices.

Although the inhabitants of such houses held no attraction for Marcel Proust, he mentions the bordellos of the Belle Epoque frequently in **A la recherche du temps perdu.** To demonstrate his friendship for one madam, the narrator gives her some of the furniture he has inherited from his Aunt Léonie. He suffers like a true martyr when he discovers the use the girls are making of his pious and virtuous aunt's divan. Proust also gives a lively description of a sumptuous seaside brothel in Normandy where the Baron de Charlus tries to find his close friend Morel, in one of the funniest passages in **The Cities of the Plain.** He writes of the "stream of announcements and awards made by an old 'assistant matron' in a very brown wig, her face crackled with the gravity of a Spanish attorney or priest, who kept shouting at every minute in a voice of thunder, ordering the doors to be alternately opened and shut, like a policeman regulating the flow of traffic: 'Take this gentleman to twenty-eight, the Spanish room.' 'Let no more in.' 'Open the door again, these gentlemen want Mademoiselle Noémie. She's expecting them in the Persian parlor' " **(Cities of the Plain).**

The madam, also known as the landlady, the Lady Pimp, played the main role in a house's reputation, its orderly management. The job called for many and contradictory qualifications. She had to be cordial and even subservient with the clients, hard and stubborn, even rude, to the girls—who were nevertheless her former colleagues. She had to be as supple and diplomatic with the customers as she was authoritarian and tyrannical with the staff. A madam worth her salt had to be tactful, discreet, modest, and versed in every taste and perversion. Some names are left us: Mademoiselle Camélia of the Montyon, Madame Gaby of the Moulins, Madame Marthe of the Chabanais.

When I visited the most luxurious of these houses in 1926—I was, alas! unable to get permission to take pictures—it was already less a "house of illusion" than a venerable museum, and it's a pity it wasn't classified as an historical monument, for that's what it really was. After the Liberation, however, France was seized with a fever of morality and virtue, and in April of 1946 the National Assembly passed a law ordering the closing of the brothels. It was also in 1946 that the historical treasures of the Chabanais—chandeliers, tapestries, Venetian mirrors, and Edward VII's weird chair—were all sold at auction.

Shortly before the Phony War, a new establishment, designed to outdo the Chabanais in luxury and fantasy, was opened at Number 4 Rue de Hanovre, just a few steps from the Opéra. In fact, this new house, called the Acropolis, replaced the Colbert, which had occupied the same site. There was a vast fresco, covering an entire wall of the main salon, of the ancient Athenian citadel on its rock, at the base of which was disposed a group of beautiful, scantily clad courtesans, some lying about, some standing or gamboling. And the same girls, in the flesh, wearing the same diaphanous veils, stood in groups around the Greco-Roman salon, with its colonnaded galleries built around a dance floor made of glass transparent as jade, which was lit from below. The bodies of these naked dancers, clad only in long floating veils, took on singular outlines in the erotic lighting. Men in tuxedos or evening dress sat around small tables under the arches—Parisian industrialists, fabric tycoons from the north, and, above all, silk manufacturers from Lyons—drinking iced champagne and surrounded by hordes of Greek hetaeras. The film world was also drawn to the Acropolis: producers, actors, directors, screenwriters. Michel Simon roomed and boarded there for months at a time.

One day I was given a tour by the fashionably dressed woman who ran the house. A world tour! Since some of the more exotic rooms were occupied, I didn't see the Chinese, Persian, or Turkish salons. But I got a look at the Virgin's Room—all in white, lace, and immaculate muslins. On the mantel-piece under a glass bell was a garland of orange blossoms, and next to it a bridal veil. The imaginative could spend their wedding night there . . . My guide also led me to the Desert Room. There one made love in an Arab tent on a soft pile of Oriental rugs. And during one's transports, it was possible to contemplate desert sands, a pink sky, and a distant caravan passing on the horizon. The diorama and its clever lighting made the illusion complete . . . And the Chamber of Mirrors! Proust must have been thinking of it when he described a room "in which the mirrors decorating it were disposed so that they seemed to reflect thirty others . . . giving the impression that the space around one [Saint-Loup is the character in the room] was multiplied . . ." **(The Guermantes Way)**. The Chamber of Mirrors in the Acropolis was an even more resounding success. All the walls and the ceiling were covered with mirrors set slightly askew, making the entwined bodies visible from all sides, reflected a thousand times. Multiplying the image of an embrace, they gave the impression of a multitude of bodies imprisoned in rock crystal, struggling and locked together in the facets of the mirrors with their blueish, purplish glitter. I also saw the torture chamber of a medieval castle. Fake flames licked the fake logs in the immense fireplace, and among the weapons and tools there was a wooden crucifix, life-size, which was tilted slightly backward. The person being crucified—woman or man depending on whether the customer was a sadist or masochist—could be hung on it and fastened down with handcuffs. It had one unique feature: at the trunk of the cross, where the legs would lie, it was divided and could be opened up to crotch level; by working a crank, the legs could be spread apart. And beyond a certain angle, screams of pain and supplications would fill the room . . . All of these reconstructions had been carried out with incredible taste and luxury. Hundreds of millions of francs had been spent. The Acropolis even had its erotic "black museum" where hundreds of valuable works, like Hokusai and Utamaro prints, were on view, along with Beardsley's marvelous drawings.

An important date in the history of Montparnasse was the opening of the Sphinx on the Boulevard Edgar-Quinet. Hundreds of artists had been invited, and the champagne flowed like water. The main salon was like a café, but in the background, under a waterfall, was a glittering statue of a golden sphinx—the only luxury in the bordello. For this house broke with the usual tradition: heavy curtains, red velvet sofas, walls covered with fabrics . . . At the Sphinx, everything was enameled, waxed, white, clean, functional, hygienic. It was like an operating room. There was another innovation: the men could bring their wives and children. Going to the Sphinx was like a family outing. The little boys would stare wide-eyed at the sylphs offering their charms, weaving stark naked in and out among the tables. A foretaste of the sex education of the future. For these children, the mystery had gone out of the huge numerals, the closed shutters, Woman, before they reached puberty. There were other bordellos that welcomed couples, who came out of curiosity and didn't go upstairs. And sometimes drinks at these houses were more profitable than tricks. Such was the case at the café-bordellos in the Saint-Denis area, and above all one in the Rue Sainte-Apolline, which was packed every night.

However, the most flourishing whorehouses in Paris were the ones known in slang as the "slaughterhouses," like the Bon Acceuil in the Boulevard de la Villette, the Flower Basket in the Boulevard de la Chapelle, the Eden in the Rue de Lappe, the Sun, Rue Caron, the Moulin Galant, Rue de Fourcy, also known as the Fourcy. These last two, in the Saint-Paul quarter, frequented mainly by North Africans, were dimestores of sex. Every movement there was calculated, measured, tailored, charged for, as in an assembly plant. When I went in one night, I couldn't believe my eyes. Like a descent into hell, like the abjection of love . . . In a suffocating haze of smoke so dense that the end of the room was invisible, there appeared gradually out of the crowded darkness a long line of men along one wall, all dressed in black, and along the other wall a line of naked girls, some of whom wore half-open red satin kimonos to conceal a scarred breast or an appendectomy. And these two long lines advanced together, giving off a smell of sweat, tobacco, jasmine, hair oil, garlic, soap, mint, anise, antiseptic—mixed with the spicy scents and unpleasant odors of an Arab souk—to meet at the counter behind which the madam sat enthroned.

The men were not allowed to pick and choose; their partner was theirs by chance. Once they had joined up before the counter, at the head of the procession, they paid the fixed price—five francs for room, trick, and tip, plus twenty-five centimes for the towel. The cash register never stopped ringing and the pile of towels was constantly replenished. No sooner would a man get his ticket—less than no time—than the girl opposite him in the line would already be leading him off. At the Moulin Galant, there were sixty women making up this parade of love, climbing up and down the steep stairs several dozen times a day, from two in the afternoon until four in the morning. And the crowds on the weekends! There was no time to catch one's breath, to take a minute's rest. In these "slaughterhouses," it was not unusual for a diligent girl, working on the Lord's Day, to pick up a clean towel forty or even fifty times in twenty-four hours—she was aptly called a "hustler."

Suzy

Suzy was the name of a small brothel in the Quartier Latin, on the Rue Grégoire-de-Tours. At night, with its colored windows, it looked like a chapel lit up for midnight mass. The owners of these small houses often seemed determined to give them a religious character; in another modest "house of illusion," on the Rue Monsieur-le-Prince, the girls paraded on a black and white tiled floor in an austere, medieval crypt, beneath vaults like those in a Romanesque cloister. In their gossamer tunics, they were more like the vestal virgins in some cult of Eros than like the staff of a Parisian whorehouse.

There were two kinds of bordellos: those in which clients were received in a public salon, and those in which each client was met separately, to respect his anonymity. In the latter, there could be a whole system of sliding doors, curtains, trap doors (a system Leonardo da Vinci had ingeniously worked out long before) to protect one customer from ever meeting another. Suzy was one of the discreet houses that guaranteed the anonymity of its guests. Even priests got in and out without being seen or recognized. Of course, bordellos

with salons had their advantages: one could look without being obliged to make love, and if one wanted to make love, a partner could be chosen at leisure.

At Suzy, a bell went off as the client opened the door, and he found himself in a kind of booth, as though he had gone to vote. The madam appeared with a wide, salacious grin. She would clap her hands and call out, "Choosing time, ladies!" All the girls who weren't otherwise occupied would remove their dressing gowns, their kimonos, pell-mell, and arrive in the simplest of apparel, whereupon they would form a **tableau vivant**: the shortest, sometimes kneeling, in front, the others standing behind them. The visitor could thus make a considered choice among the bodies before him. Yet how was it possible to take in ten female bodies at a glance, to judge their good qualities, their imperfections? Embarrassed, the client would make his choice almost at random, based on a smile, the firmness of a breast, the curve of a thigh. How would Paris have been able to pick Aphrodite from among the Three Graces had he been given so short a time? The client, having caught his breath, his decision made—and already being called "Sweetheart"—would then allow himself to be led up the stairs by his short-term fiancée, a set of towels under his arm.

From two in the afternoon until two in the morning, the routine would go on. While waiting, the girls would be terribly bored, and would give themselves manicures, gossip, play cards. Alas, they rarely finished a hand, since each time the bell rang and "Choosing time!" rang out, they had to jump up and rush off. And each time, they would return one less.

They often listened to music. The madam was a music lover, an Opéra-Comique addict. She adored the great arias from **La Fille de Madame Angot, La Traviata, The Barber of Seville**. One day, she invited me to spend an evening behind the scenes at Suzy. It was her saint's day. She served champagne and petits fours. And then she confided, "We've got a fine clientele. Mainly merchants from the neighborhood. They're very upstanding people. And some out-of-towners, too, regular customers. Believe me, most of them come here not so much for the 'fun' as to forget, to get away from their worries. They like to get attention, to be fussed over, to be caressed . . . They love to talk about their lives, their wives, their children, to show us pictures . . . You know, they've worked hard, they've had successful lives, earned a lot of money, and—well—they're bored. Believe me. They come here to forget and to get drunk . . ."

We were chatting in a room on the ground floor which was reserved for the staff. The "work rooms" were upstairs. So where was all the laughter, the sound of voices, coming from?

"That's next door," the madam explained. "We have a little salon . . . it's for good clients who just want to drink some champagne with the girls. There's a restaurant owner from the Boulevard Saint-Germain in there at the moment. His place is closed on Wednesdays, and every Tuesday evening he comes in . . . He could go to the theater or to a music hall with his wife and family, but he prefers spending Tuesday nights with us. He reserves three girls and the small salon. He drinks a few bottles of champagne with them. There's a man who knows how to live! He doesn't care about the expense. And when he's completely drunk, he passes out . . . At six in the morning, every Wednesday now for years, his wife sends a taxi to bring him home. It's always the same taxi, the same driver, the same time. He's really an excellent client! But, poor man, he's so unhappy . . ."

Suddenly we heard screams. What was going on? Worried, the madam cocked her ear to listen. Then there was an awful commotion, as if the house were falling down—the sound of furniture being overturned, glass breaking. The madam rushed to the scene, followed by the harem. And what a sight! Everything was topsy-turvy, tables and chairs thrown about, bottles and glasses broken. The ice from the champagne bucket was all over the floor. Lying on his back on a divan, naked as a jaybird, his immense paunch flopping over on either side, was a huge man, twitching and kicking, his legs in the air, family jewels in the middle, like an immense baby being powdered after his bath. It was indescribable. Then I saw a trickle of blood running down one of the girl's breasts.

"The pig bit me," she screamed, trying to grab hold of his feet. "The rotten pig!"

With another girl's help, she threw her weight on his legs to hold them down, while a third girl, who was wearing a pink ribbon around her waist,

tried to catch his arms. And all the time, he was yelling "Let me go, get away, go to hell!"

His body gradually slid off the sofa and all at once he fell onto the floor in a heap, bumping his head.

"My God, what are you doing? Stop it! Stop it!" the madam shouted, pulling at her hair. "You're killing my best client!"

ARTISTS' DANCES IN MONTPARNASSE

NOVELISTS and chroniclers of all nationalities have given innumerable descriptions of the famous cafés at the crossroads of the Rue Vavin: the Dôme, the Rotonde, the Coupole, the Select—and of the life and work of the artists who lived in Montparnasse. Here, therefore, I want to evoke a lesser-known place, one that disappeared long ago, where the bohemians of Montparnasse held their parties: the Bal Bullier. It was on the border of Montparnasse and the Quartier Latin, across from the restaurant called the Closerie des Lilas, and it was opened at the same time as the Jardin de Paris on the Champs-Elysées, the Casino on the Rue Blanche and the Moulin Rouge on the Place Blanche in Montmartre. Frequented for the most part by students and ladies of easy virtue, this ballroom was also where the artists of Montparnasse—known in those days as "the Horde"—held their big costume parties, evenings of gaiety and fantasy. These fêtes were also attended by tuxedoed bourgeois eager to rub elbows with Bohemia and to help in picking the most beautiful model. The queen of these wild Montparnasse artists' balls was a beautiful redhead with a violent, volcanic temper named Madeleine Lequeux, known to all as "the Pantheress"; I took her picture seated among the musicians in the band.

LE BAL NÈGRE IN THE RUE BLOMET

AFTER the First World War, along with the Charleston, the beguine, and the shimmy, Parisians—particularly Parisian women—discovered the Bal Nègre in the Rue Blomet. As though the carnage of the war had inspired a sudden sexual frenzy, white women—drunk on their own bodies and forgetting that contact with a Negro had once been shocking—were irresistibly drawn to the Vth arrondissement, the Harlem of Paris. Every evening, luxurious automobiles unloaded hordes of elegant society neurotics, all of them avid to throw themselves—quite literally—into the arms of handsome, athletic Senegalese, Antillan, Guinean, or Sudanese men.

A kind of hysterical sorcery permeated this night club, which throbbed to the beat of syncopated music: shoulders shook, breasts quivered, hips undulated. It was like some voodoo rite. Glued together, belly to belly, breast to breast, the couples gyrated and pulsed as though they were naked together in bed.

The passion for Negroes reached its peak around 1925, with the arrival in France of the American Negro Dance Company and the resounding success of

Josephine Baker. Taking advantage of the craze, other Negro night clubs soon opened in Montparnasse and Montmartre, the Boule Blanche, the Cabane Cubaine, and many more. The whites gradually grew disenchanted with the Bal Nègre in the Rue Blomet.

KIKI OF MONTPARNASSE

A love child, she had the right background . . . Her mother had had six children, all of unknown fathers, and she had abandoned all of them in her native Burgundy to follow her last lover to Paris. Little Alice Prin, the future Kiki of Montparnasse, received—along with her illegitimate brothers and sisters—an undisciplined upbringing from her peasant grandmother, kindly, devoted, but overworked. And then one day her mother remembered her and sent for Alice to come to Paris. For her education? For amusement? No, not at all. To put her to work. She started out in a printing shop, went on to a shoe factory, and then to a florist on the Rue Mouffetard. It was on this picturesque street that an old sculptor hired her as his model. She was only fourteen—"It bothered me a little to take off my clothes," she wrote in her **Memoirs**, "but since it was the custom . . ." Upon learning of this, her mother burst into the artist's studio in a rage, called her daughter a whore, and disowned her. Thus it was that Kiki, alone in Paris, without money or a roof over her head, turned up in Montparnasse one day earning her living by posing for painters.

She was a beautiful dark-haired girl, whose beauty flouted every classical canon: a bird's head with a funny pointed nose was perched on a long neck; her face was framed with black hair greased down like a boy's which fell over her forehead in bangs; beneath high, arched brows, her eyes, wide and amber colored, were shadowed with long, thick eyelashes; she had a tiny heart-shaped mouth with full lips like Yvette Guilbert's, and her mischievous smile revealed sparkling teeth. A young Burgundian with pearly skin, she was voluptuous, with a wonderful figure: high, pointed breasts, broad hips, thin waist, long, firm legs. A fascinating flower sprung up from the Parisian cobblestones, Kiki radiated seductiveness, life. And she communicated to others her joy, her pleasure in being alive. Her voluptuous glance, her provocative body, revealed an insatiable sensuality. In fact, Kiki was always **naked**, body and soul, totally naughty, totally immodest. When she was young, she was already showing her breasts . . . for three francs. Beneath the most fashionable clothes, she wore neither panties nor bra, but simply black garters on her white thighs. When she bent over, she revealed her full bosom, and her skirt went up and down like a theater curtain. One thing bothered her, however: she had no pubic hair. So sometimes, when she was posing for someone she didn't know, she would draw on fake hair with a piece of charcoal. Kiki raised immodesty to an art. Her wit was equally uncorseted. Totally spontaneous, frank without the slightest trace of hypocrisy, she called things by their names. She never avoided vulgar words, but when she spoke them in her fresh, innocent voice, they lost all their vulgarity and even took on a kind of nobility.

So quite naturally she became the undisputed queen of that kingdom of freedom and frankness that was Montparnasse at its height. No one symbolized the quarter's nonconformity better than this delicious figurehead of independence. Thus, for twenty years, Kiki's name was spread throughout the world, forever associated with the magic name of Montparnasse.

Kiki had great wit and many talents. On the terrace of the Dôme, the Sélect, or the Rotonde, she was always surrounded by admirers, both male and female. No one wanted to miss a word of her wild remarks, her comic stories—most of them off-color—which she could reel off all night long. Upon her arrival in Montparnasse, Foujita had made her his favorite model: "One day she came into my studio in the Rue Delambre," he wrote, "naked beneath her coat. . . ." The Japanese painter adored her, though she was never his mistress, and when she died, he made a point of accompanying his former model to the cemetery. She also posed for Van Dongen, for Per Krogh, and especially for Kisling, whose friends also called him Kiki. For a few years, she was the lover of Man Ray, the American Dadaist photographer and painter of the Roaring Twenties, and she was also the star of his short film, **L'Étoile de Mer.** It was a stormy, volcanic love affair, punctuated with fights, breakups, violent, jealous public scenes with blows and nail-scratching, followed by reconciliations. It lasted for six years. When she felt something for an artist, Kiki would move into his studio, cook for him—Burgundian cooking, of course—and share his bed. But she never gave herself for money. Among her friends was an accordion player who accompanied her on her singing engagements. Around 1932, she sang at the Cabaret des Fleurs in the Rue Montparnasse, which is where I photographed her. One night, after a huge dinner, I also took several pictures at her home: the Three Graces of Montparnasse on a sofa with their dogs: Thérèse Treize de Caro, Lily, and Kiki.

She began her career as a singer at the Jockey-Bar, the first night club in Montparnasse, in an old, one-story house. The figures of cowboys and Indians on the façade had been painted by Hilary Hiler, an American. Inside, the walls were covered with old posters, and on the narrow dance floor, couples of every nationality jammed together to the beat of jazz. So many people crammed into such a small place! It was more like a saloon in the gold rush than a Parisian night club. In this hot, colorful—and smoky—atmosphere, Kiki sang nightly in her harsh voice her repertoire of Rabelaisian songs: "Les Trois Orfèvres," "Nini peau de chien," and many more in that vein. It was there, one winter's day in 1924, the day after my arrival in Paris, that I heard her sing for the first time in the total silence of the club: "Les filles de Camaret se disent toutes vierges . . ." ["The girls of Camaret say they are all virgins"].

She sang barrack-room ballads with deadpan humor and a completely innocent face. A true **diseuse**, her voice pleasant and true, she cast a spell

with every word. A smile would appear on her lips only at the end of the last couplet! The Jockey had other singers: Marcelle, Chiffonette, but the public wanted Kiki. People came from far and wide to hear her, and other night clubs tried to hire her away. Once she appeared at the Boeuf sur le Toit, Jean Cocteau's fashionable Right Bank cabaret. Then someone offered her a contract to go to America. No sooner had she landed in New York, however, than she re-embarked for Paris. Outside her own quarter, she felt like an exile, her exuberant personality lost its bearings.

One day she began to draw and paint. The exhibition of these naïve pictures, with their lively, fresh colors, was a big event in Montparnasse. They were all sold on the day of the opening. She wrote her **Memoirs.** In short, racy, incisive sentences, she told about her hard rural childhood, her failures at school, her fights with the nuns, her Parisian days of hunger, nights without a roof over her head, her love affairs, her life as a model in Montparnasse. A moving, gay book, with an astonishing naturalness, a ring of truth. And it was a success: even the English version, which was published by Helena Rubinstein's husband Titus, sold out quickly. Unfortunately, however, devoid as she was of any practical sense, Kiki had no idea how to exploit her many talents. She lacked the ambition to be a star. She tossed all her gifts generously to the winds.

And she came to a bad end. Like all the victims of the Montparnasse poison—which acted as a stimulant in small doses, but was fatal in large ones—Kiki began to drink, to take drugs. Most of the victims of those mad years went away to die. Kiki stayed on the bridge and went down with the ship. Drunken, staggering, stuffed with drugs, suffering from dropsy, which she did nothing to cure, she dragged herself miserably from one café to another. Outlandishly made up, thick layers of mascara around her eyes, she began to look like the Môme Bijou. For everyone who had known her in her glory, it was terribly sad to watch her downfall. And when she died in 1953, the entire quarter mourned its queen. It was almost as though the soul of Montparnasse were being buried with her in the cemetery at Thiais. The Montparnasse of the great days did not survive her.

IN THE WINGS AT THE FOLIES-BERGÈRE

ONE winter day in 1932, I got permission to take photographs backstage at the Folies-Bergère. It was a rare privilege, since the management had always forbidden anything that might impede the working of that vast pleasure machine in which every step, every movement, was planned and calculated, timed to the second. The magic of a great music hall is not what appears on the stage, rich and dazzling as that may be. The magic—full of surprises, full of the unexpected—occurs backstage. The combination of naked dancers, stage-hands, beplumed showgirls, firemen, eighteenth-century lords and ladies, transforms the wings into a fantastic dream. The curtains as they go up and down, the constantly shifting scenery, afford fleeting, unexpected glimpses onto the stage with its trap doors, mirrors, projectors—all the complex machinery that can in a few seconds change the set from an aquarium full of naiads into a rainbow bearing naked Amazons, a beach at Juan-les-Pins, a cage full of wild beasts—a bevy of beautiful girls—or into a gigantic spider web where a naked Circe lures her victims. The heated and feverish atmosphere of the dressing rooms while the girls are making their twenty costume changes, the way they clatter up and down the stairs, the machinists' bridge with its forest of ropes—each with its secret name—the dizzying views down onto the stage, new and astonishing perspectives at every moment . . .

THE BAL DES QUAT 'Z ARTS

THERE were two balls in those days that were completely uninhibited: one for med students and the other for art students. The first of them, the Interns' Ball, was held in the fall, in September or October, to coincide with the final day of the hospital exams. It was private, limited to members of the Medical College. On that evening, in the entrance halls of each of the larger Paris hospitals—the Hôtel-Dieu, Beaujon, Bichat, Cochin, Lariboisière, Laënnec, La Salpêtrière, and so on—there would be a dinner for the medical students and a few younger members of the staff. And a few uninhibited girls. There was eating, drinking, and song:

> Saint Eloi n'est pas mort!
> Saint Eloi n'est pas mort!
> Car il bande encore!
> Car il bande encore!

(Saint Eloi [patron of medicine] isn't dead! He can still get it up!)

Lots of smutty jokes were told. Just to break the ice, everyone was naked. Some covered their bodies with glitter—a mixture of gold dust and beer, which wouldn't asphyxiate the skin and was easy to wash off. Around midnight, closed buses would arrive to pick up the med students at each hospital, and take them to the Salle Wagram near the Étoile, which had been rented for a night of debauchery. The "artistic" part of the program consisted of electing a Queen of the Ball, and a parade of Rabelaisian floats. Some represented giant phalluses around which fauns and satyrs frolicked and ravished gorgeous nymphs. Although the ball was strictly limited to the world of medicine, there were exceptions made for women. These "volunteers," who were neither female doctors nor students, were girls between twenty and thirty years old determined to spend the night on their backs with their legs in the air. They often arrived in Paris from great distances, with visions of passing from one private box to another—each hospital had its own—from one pair of arms to another, from midnight until dawn.

The Bal des Quat'z Arts—the art students' ball—took place in the spring. Although the theme was changed every year—Incas, Aztecs, Phoenicians, Egyptians, Gauls— the costumes were always practically nonexistent. There wasn't much fuss about historical authenticity. The men wore decorated jockstraps or Roman tunics, the women draped themselves in thin, transparent muslin to reveal their nakedness. They made up for the lack of clothes with their hats and head ornaments: turbans, tarbooshes, pointed hats, pagan jewelry, make-up. Everyone, male and female, was covered with vivid colored paint: red, bronze, even gold and silver. Their faces and eyes were smeared with burnt cork. Henri Matisse, one of the few great painters to have attended the École des Beaux-Arts, had attended a ball when he was a student. One day he told me: "The Bal des Quat'z Arts was the one time in my life when all I possessed was my bedsheet, draped around me like a burnoose, a red cord tied around my head, and burnt cork outlining my eyes. I've never forgotten the smell of that burnt cork . . ."

The ball, named for the four plastic arts—architecture, engraving, painting, and sculpture—was much more than a ball; it was like a Roman Saturnalia, where every license was permitted. Unlike the Bal de l'Internat, it took place mainly out of doors, in the streets. When the big day came—a fine day in May—the Rue Bonaparte would turn into a beehive. The action began in the huge courtyard of the art school. From the Quai Malaquais to the church of

Saint-Germain-des-Prés, the entire quarter would seethe with excitement. Happy throngs of young people dressed as Adam and Eve would spread out through the streets, brandishing spears, arrows, cardboard shields. They sang, they yelled, they shouted war cries. They invaded café terraces, made riotous sorties into the Deux-Magots, the Café de Flore, the Brasserie Lipp. They made free with the girls and molested passers-by, flouted the police, provoked the taxi drivers, stopped cars and buses, and often blocked traffic completely. Just like the old days in Rome, when bands of drunken slaves, wearing the insignia of ex-bondsmen, would spread out through the city during the Saturnalia, when normal life was suspended. Under the benign eye of the authorities, they were allowed to foment disorder and commit thousands of prohibited acts. So, too, the French police respected this right to licentiousness, and for one night, under their tolerant protection, there was a return to an earlier civilization.

The high point of the day was the famous "uprising": the traversal of Paris from the Left Bank to the Right, from the Rue Bonaparte to the Avenue de Wagram. Some paraded along the quays, others down the Boulevard Saint-Germain. Passing through the Place de la Concorde, they proceeded up the Champs-Elysées. It was unforgettable to see this wild, naked horde, fairly drunk, as—to the horror of uninformed foreign visitors—it invaded the cafés on the avenue, kissing women and producing general panic. The parents of a young English friend of mine, who were making their first visit to Paris and had planned to spend a week, arrived in town on the day of the Quat'z Arts Ball and checked into a hotel on the Rue Bonaparte. An incredible mob was howling, rioting, and gesticulating in front of their hotel. The English couple had always been wary of Paris and of the French—"dangerous and mad," full of debauchery, vice, perversion—and Paris exceeded everything they had imagined! Besieged as they were, they were so terrified by the frenzy, so shocked and scandalized by the breasts, buttocks, and costumes, that without even unpacking their bags, they fled back to London on the spot, swearing never to return to this accursed, devil-worshiping city . . .

The art students' ball was also held in the Salle Wagram, decorated for the occasion by the leading student in the school. It too had its parade of floats and its contest for the most beautiful model. Borne in on platforms by four burly

fellows, the candidates would be exhibited stark naked before the jury. The intimate part of the ball, however—like that of the Interns'—took place on the side. Each art studio had its private loge, a kind of grotto for drinking and lovemaking. Each student would escort—or carry—his conquest or prey there . . . A special room was set aside for the "cadavers," but this slang expression, which usually means "empty bottles," had a special meaning on this occasion. It signified the bodies of all those handsome Aztecs, Incas, or Gauls, drained, passed out, and laid low from fatigue, lovemaking, and alcohol, deposited unceremoniously on the floor. Come dawn, many of those valiant warriors would be laid out side by side, dead to the world, sleeping soundly.

The warriors of the exhausted army who were still able to move—now without their staffs, their lances, or their armor—would set off for the Etoile. And then there would be the morning "descent" down the deserted Champs-Elysées and the traditional regenerative dip in the fountains at the Rond-Point, and then the fountains on the Place de la Concorde, amid the Sirens, the Tritons, and the Naiads, while the streetcleaners, with brooms and water, arrived to take possession of the still sleeping city . . .

SODOM
AND GOMORRAH

Le Monocle

Although Paris in the thirties had a few intimate bars where women could meet among themselves, the sumptuous, specialized night clubs of the Champs-Elysées, Montmartre, or Montparnasse—like Frida, Quolibet, Moune, Carroll's Club, and the other hideouts reserved exclusively for the "weaker" sex—did not exist in those days. The Monocle, on the Boulevard Edgar-Quinet, was one of the first temples of Sapphic love, as famous in its day as its neighbor, the fashionable Montparnasse bordello known as Le Sphinx.

I was introduced to this capital of Gomorrah one evening by Fat Claude, who was an habituée of such places. From the owner, known as Lulu de Montparnasse, to the barmaid, from the waitresses to the hat-check girl, all

the women were dressed as men, and so totally masculine in appearance that at first glance one thought they were men. A tornado of virility had gusted through the place and blown away all the finery, all the tricks of feminine coquetry, changing women into boys, gangsters, policemen. Gone the trinkets, veils, ruffles! Pleasant colors, frills! Obsessed by their unattainable goal to be men, they wore the most somber uniforms: black tuxedos, as though in mourning for their ideal masculinity . . . And of course their hair—woman's crowning glory, abundant, waved, sweet-smelling, curled—had also been sacrificed on Sappho's altar. The customers of Le Monocle wore their hair in the style of a Roman emperor or Joan of Arc. Even their perfumes—frowned on here—had been replaced by Lord knows what weird scents, more like amber or incense than roses and violets.

As I watched these women dancing slowly together, pressed close against each other, their breasts touching, I thought of Marcel Proust, of his jealousy, his sick curiosity about the foreign pleasures of Gomorrah. The fact that Albertine had been unfaithful to the narrator with a woman bothered him far less than the kind of pleasures she had experienced with her partner. "What can they really be feeling?" he continually wondered.

Sometimes a few outsiders would try to get into the fold. Some girls for whom lesbianism seemed less of a risk than an affair with a man would disguise themselves as tomboys in order to earn a little money. However, the masculine female clientele looked at these fake lesbians, sized them up, judged them, and unmasked them with a glance. For that matter, one-night stands didn't interest them. These women, their passions slower to ignite, generally looked for more devotion and fidelity in their love affairs than do pederasts, most of whom cruise a lot and are often content with a quick trick. In the female bars, there was also more discretion and probity than in male gathering places. Evenings at Le Monocle never got as frenetic as those at the Carrousel or Madame Arthur's, the capitals of Sodom in those days.

Lulu de Montparnasse, the owner of Le Monocle, was a masterful woman with a husky build, whose stentorian voice filled the room. She left Montparnasse a few years later for Montmartre, and raised the standard of Sapphism in the Rue Pigalle.

The Ball at "Magic City"

IN 1933, I attended a strange ball: the last of the big homosexual balls at
Magic City. The cream of Parisian inverts was to meet there, without distinc-
tion as to class, race, or age. And every type came, faggots, cruisers, chickens,
old queens, famous antique dealers and young butcherboys, hairdressers and
elevator boys, well-known dress designers and drag queens, the Duchess Zoé,
the Peruvian, Mimosa and Peaches, Mignon and Divine, the Blonde and
Notre-Dame-des-Fleurs, the Baron de Charlus and the tailor Jupien, every
Albert and André—metamorphosed for this great night into Andrée and
Albertine . . .

They arrived in small groups, after having emptied the closets of the fairer
sex: dresses and corsets, hats, lingerie, wigs, jewelry, necklaces, mascara,
creams and perfumes . . . Everyone wore silk flowers, garlands, ropes of
pearls, feathers, trinkets . . . Of course most of them were in dressmaking,
lacemaking, furs, hairdressing—creators of hats, ribbons, embroidery, fabrics, laces . . . Almost all of them had devoted their lives to dressing, beauti-
fying, deifying women, making them seductive and attractive for others to
love—for they certainly didn't.

Every entrance and every costume gave rise to shrieks of surprise, cries of
astonishment, of joy. They embraced, they showered each other with compli-
ments, they admired and kissed. They camped and teased each other with
squeals of delight. An immense, warm, impulsive fraternity. There were
monstrous couples, grotesque couples, some were surprising and even heart-
warming. Two young men wrapped in each other's arms had—to demonstrate
the perfect union of their souls, their bodies—dressed in a single suit: one was
wearing the jacket, with his legs and buttocks naked; the other wore the
pants, his torso and feet bare, since he had given his boyfriend the only pair of
shoes.

Most of the couples were less well matched, however. Mature men accompanied by youths in drag were the rule. With hair by Antoine, clothes by
Lanvin or Madeleine Vionnet, the great couturiers of the period, some of these

ephebes on the arms of their rich protectors were extremely beautiful and elegant. They had figures like fashion models. And I saw many enigmatic, unidentifiable creatures, floating between the poorly drawn barrier between the sexes in a sort of no man's land. There were long, fragile necks, smooth doll-like faces, peaches and cream complexions, platinum hair set off by a camellia or a red carnation. And what about the low necklines that often revealed the swelling of breasts? And the dresses designed to accentuate the bosom? Were they fake breasts? In those days, they were already making them out of rubber, built into a brassiere. Or were they real breasts, hermaphrodite breasts? Hormone treatments hadn't yet been invented, nor had operations to alter sex surgically . . . These creatures who lent such an ambiguous tone to the evening were obviously the forerunners of the Coccinelles and the Bambis—the great contemporary Parisian drag queens—today's celebrated stars of Parisian night life, appearing in so many all-male night clubs.

With humor, with self-mockery, many "old aunties" dressed the part. In fact, noisy and picturesque, they gave life to the evening. With their gem-laden fingers, they would lift their ruffled skirts and petticoats like French cancan dancers, revealing their feminine undergarments: silk slips, lace panties, embroidered jockstraps, garters around their muscular, hairy calves. And the curls, the blond wigs that hid balding heads! Pigtails, curls falling into mascaraed eyes, the pupils dilated with belladonna. Here and there were heads crowned with huge old-fashioned bonnets loaded with feathers or ribbons, or the enormous cartwheel hats of the Gay Nineties. And these middle-aged nellies in their finery and their glad-rags would utter piercing shrieks, join hands, and dance wildly together. There were no indiscreet onlookers here to make them uneasy. No threatening opprobrium from "normal" men, no humiliating female disdain, no inquisitorial vice squad surveillance looking for outrages to public decency. On that night, the "love that dares not speak its name" said it loud and clear, shouted it from the rooftops . . .

The Bal
de la Montagne Sainte-Geneviève

LOCATED on the summit of the hill behind the Panthéon, across from the École Polytechnique, the dance hall of the Montagne Sainte-Geneviève seemed to be like any ordinary dance hall. Little red lights twinkled around the entrance and inside; banquettes against the walls left space in the middle of the room for dancing. The four-man band was perched up on a tiny balcony in the Art Deco style of 1925. When the music wasn't playing, the place was like an ordinary popular dance hall, the customers chatting and sipping varicolored drinks—pink, green, purple. But when the band launched into a java, a waltz, however, the ambiguity knocked one over. On the floor were only couples of men or couples of women . . . never a woman and a man.

A century before, the Bal de la Montagne Sainte-Geneviève had been a true popular dance hall, frequented by toughs and their girls from the nearby Rue Mouffetard. Gradually, however, the female element disappeared, the "toughs" were transformed into "softs" and danced together—which led to the

establishment's being closed from time to time by the cops. There was no ban on homosexuality in France, and the police were fairly tolerant toward "special" night clubs. So long as the customers maintained a minimum of decent behavior and the management kept out minors and prohibited overly blatant cruising, the police left such places alone. However, though women had always been allowed to dance together, men doing so was one of the forbidden pleasures. It's odd that in French literature, Sapphic love has always been allowed a certain dispensation, whereas up until Gide and Proust, there was a ban on love between men. Often, the Bal de la Montagne Sainte-Geneviève was closed by the police because pairs of inverts had been caught in the act of passionate waltzes and javas.

In an attempt to mitigate the rather special atmosphere of her dance hall, the owner—an ex-movie starlette—had had the clever notion of attracting a female clientele . . . but not just any kind of woman. Although butch women repel male homosexuals and are not attracted to men, homosexual men and feminine lesbians have always felt a mutual sympathy, a kindness, toward each other. In this dance hall, Sodom and Gomorrah—or Lesbos, rather—got along beautifully together. Couples of women would drink quietly alongside couples of men and when the band struck up they would all take to the floor. Since the patroness had set up lookouts to signal the sudden arrival of the vice squad—known as "jackasses" in these circles—men were henceforth able to dance together.

The high season at this dance hall occurred at Mardi Gras and Mid-Lent. The hall would be packed with costumed customers, men dressed as women, women dressed as men, jostling each other and fighting the crush on the tiny dance floor until dawn.

One piquant note: once in a while one would see butchers from the neighborhood—rather common in appearance, but with hearts full of feminine longings—forming surprising couples. They would hold hands—thick, calloused hands—like timid children, and would waltz solemnly together, their eyes downcast, blushing wildly.

AN OPIUM DEN

As I crossed the courtyard, my nostrils picked up a bitter, sweetish odor. I rang the bell. After a long wait, the door of the isolated ground-floor studio finally opened. As the curtains were drawn aside, I found myself in the darkness of a Parisian opium den. I had met Achille S., the son of an industrial family, in Montparnasse, and he had invited me to visit his "studio," which was a hangout for opium addicts. It was not in the neighborhood of the Gare de Lyon, the Quai de Javel, or in Boulogne-Billancourt—the Chinese enclaves of Paris, little Pekings, full of retired colonials, where "puffing bamboo" was commonplace—but on the Avenue Bosquet, in the high-class Ecole Militaire district.

A few male and female silhouettes gradually emerged from the shadows, as did divans, sofas covered with brocades and velvets, and low Chinese

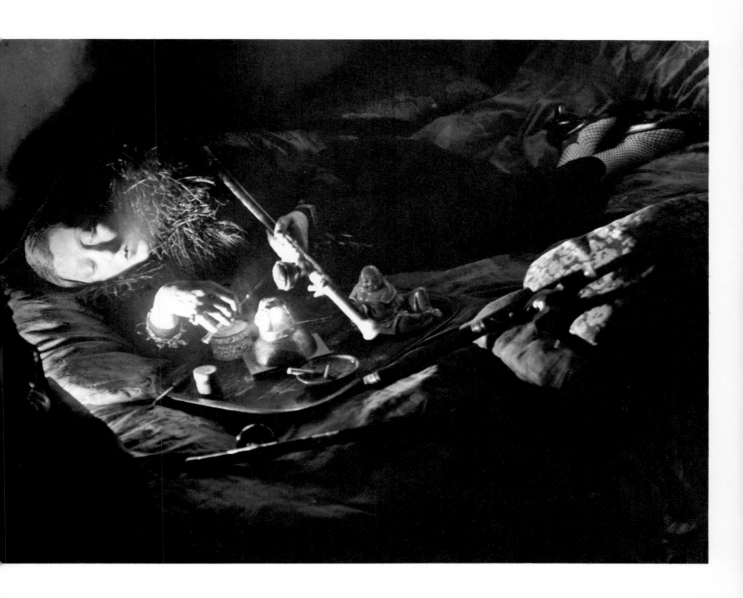

tables bearing trays loaded with pipes, lacquered boxes, and ceramic bowls; oil lamps gave off a subdued light—all the panoply of an opium den. My eyes took in Chinese vases and statues of Buddha . . .

To my great surprise, however, nobody was smoking. The whole crowd was milling around in a state of agitation.

"It's terrible, Achille," an elegant woman was exclaiming. "What will we do? Isn't there any chance of getting a pipe today? What's happened?"

"The package hasn't come yet . . . I'm dreadfully sorry," replied the master of the house in a worried voice.

"My poor Jacqueline," said the lady from Passy, turning toward her fourteen- or fifteen-year-old daughter. "The one time I promise you a pipe for your birthday— You're really out of luck, pet, the first time I've brought you here . . . And we're leaving tomorrow on a cruise. What will we do without some 'stuff,' Achille?"

Complaints, reproaches, recriminations. But Achille kept cool. He was wearing a silk tunic, and he saw to it that I put on the ritual kimono of silver or gold brocade, so as to blend in with the atmosphere. "You look like a Persian prince," he told me flatteringly, leading me to a mirror so that I could see myself in Eastern dress.

Instead of reassuring his guests, he began to initiate me into the secrets of laudanum.

"The ball of opium is heated over the flame from the **keden**, a little lamp with perfumed oil, on long steel needles, and when it is soft, the pipe is filled. In the old days, **congais**—Chinese servants—prepared the pipes with an Asiatic ceremony. Unfortunately, we don't have **congais** any more, and each smoker has to do this himself."

Achille then picked up one of the handsomest pipes, decorated with ivory and mother-of-pearl, incrusted with silver; his lamp was of jade, perhaps porcelain.

"All the pipes you see here are part of a collection I put together myself. A person has the right to have a collection of antique pipes, doesn't he? And the vice squad knows that. The first thing they look for during a search is the condition of the pipes. Are the ends plugged up, are they free of opium deposit? If so, they'll consider it a collection. If they aren't, it's an 'opium den.'

But let the detectives find any opium pots, **kedens** full of oil, any of the things you see lying around here, and you're lost . . . I know what I'm talking about . . ."

Although he was still young, Achille was an old hand, an expert. He had already been arrested several times, and had been sent to prison for drug traffic.

Among the habitués, I came across a beautiful actress and asked if I might take her picture.

"Of course! And you have my permission to print it. I'm proud to smoke . . . They say that after a while drugs, opium, will destroy you, make you thin, weaken you, ruin your mind, your memory, that it makes you stagger, gives you a yellow complexion, sunken eyes, all of that . . . Rot! Look at me. And tell me frankly, am I not beautiful and desirable? Well, let me tell you, I've smoked opium for ten years, and I'm doing all right."

Suddenly the doorbell rang. Achille carefully drew the curtains aside and checked the visitor's identity through a peephole. No, not the cops from the vice squad, but the mailman. He handed over a small registered package, as harmless looking as thousands like it mailed every day. Did it come from Smyrna, from Istanbul, Egypt, Iran, Hong Kong? Merely from Marseilles.

The mailman left and there was an outburst of joy. The stuff had arrived!

"Jacqueline, my darling, you're going to get your pipe!" the woman rejoiced, and she kissed Achille and her daughter effusively.

"Darling, I want to pay up. How many pipes do I owe you?" Achille glanced at a slate hanging on the wall. There were a dozen or so initials, followed by chalk marks put there by each client after he had smoked a pipe.

After having pocketed a wad of bills, my host took from the package a thick paste—a thousand white poppy tears coagulated and blackened by contact with the air—the black seemed almost reddish! Over an alcohol burner, he prepared the "jam." The devil's cuisine! Within a short while, his guests—or more precisely, his clients—were lying on the divans and sofas, each of them holding a droplet of opium over the **keden**'s flame. When it was heated it became smooth and brilliant, ready to be smoked.

Since every addict is a proselytizer, the actress took my arm before filling her pipe. "Come on, lie here beside me. I'll fix you a pipe. You ought to try it.

And you'll see—after all, smoking opium is a taste like any other. There's no reason not to give it a try. But above all, don't judge by the first pipe, it's always a disappointment. After three or four, then you'll tell me . . ."

The room fell silent. There was no sound but the spluttering of the drug over the flames. Prelude to euphoria. Once the burning globule was in the bowl of the pipe, only two or three puffs were needed to produce the "divine smoke."

I took a few pictures, discreetly, and left the opium imbibers to their voluptuous dreams . . .

14e ARR
RUE
ÉMILE RICHARD
PRÉPARATION
SERVICE MILITAIRE
GAITE
DE
MONTPARNASSE

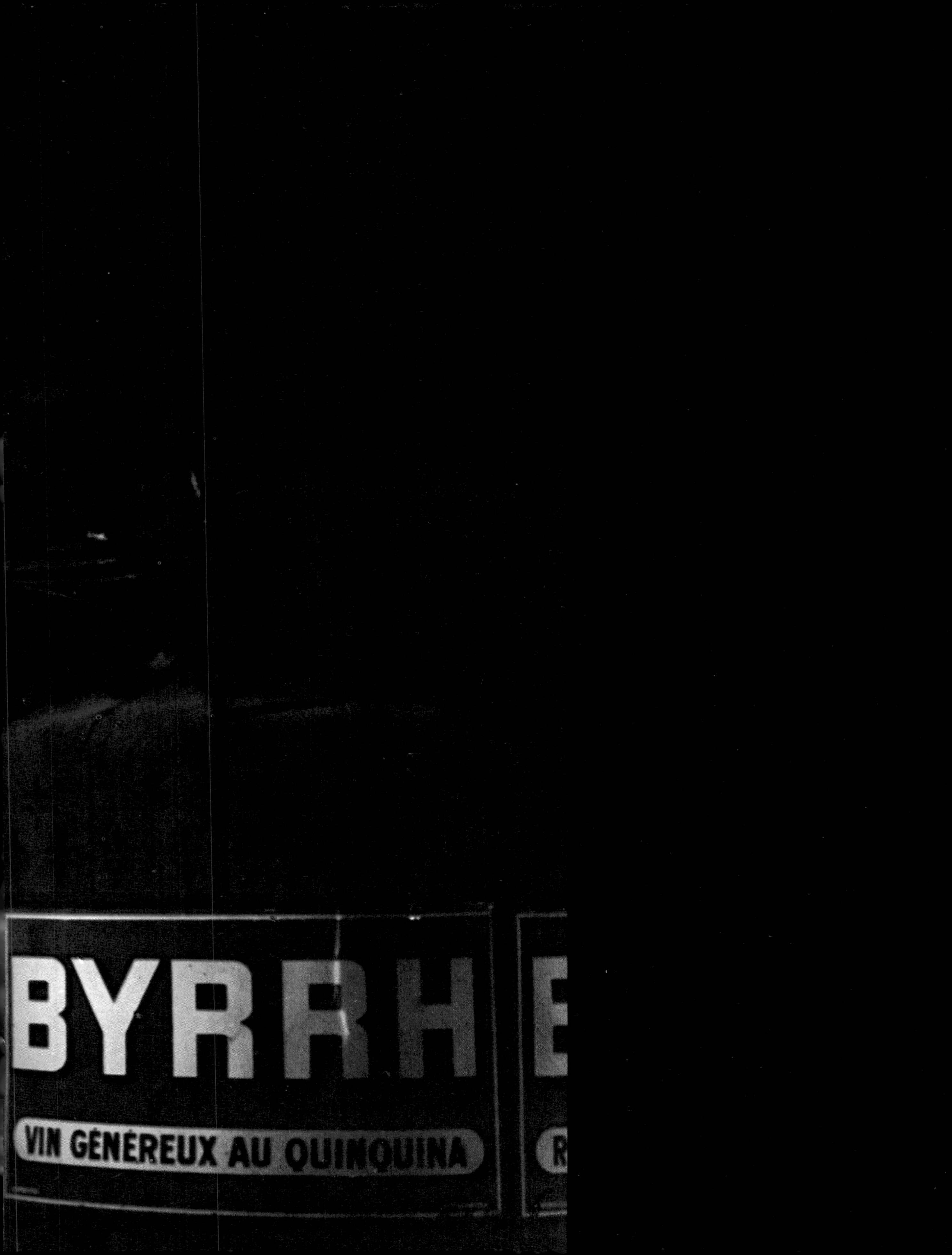
BYRRH
VIN GÉNÉREUX AU QUINQUINA

ILLUSTRATIONS

A gas company employee lighting the gas lamps on the Place de la Concorde. Paris began to be gaslit in 1838. Electricity began to be installed around the turn of the century, but in the thirties, large portions of Paris were still lit by gas (c. 1933).

The Concierge of Notre Dame

Nocturnal view from Notre Dame overlooking Paris and the Tour Saint-Jacques (1933).

Nocturnal view from Notre Dame overlooking the Hôtel-Dieu (c. 1933).

The Street Fair

Street fair on the Place d'Italie (c. 1931).

Conchita, or, Eros at the Street Fair

Dancers on display in front of their booth, Boulevard Saint-Jacques (c. 1931).

Conchita's dance at "Her Majesty, Woman," Boulevard Auguste-Blanqui (c. 1931).

Conchita on display in front of "Her Majesty, Woman."

Conchita with sailors in a café on the Place d'Italie (c. 1933).

The Human Gorilla

The Human Gorilla's wife in her "Loïe Fuller" dance, Place d'Italie (c. 1933).

The Human Gorilla with his son Peterchen in the acrobats' hotel, Boulevard Rochechouart, Montmartre (c. 1933).

A fortuneteller in her wagon, Boulevard Saint-Jacques (c. 1933).

Tarot cards, crystal ball (c. 1933).

Street fair, Place Saint-Jacques (c. 1934). (Taken from the window of my Paris apartment.)

A kiss on the giant swing, Boulevard Saint-Jacques (c. 1934).

The fourteenth of July, Place de la Contrescarpe, Montagne Sainte-Geneviève (c. 1932).

The fourteenth of July, Place de la Bastille (c. 1934).

Fireworks on the fourteenth of July, the Ile de la Cité, near Notre Dame (c. 1934).

The Last Bum of the Cour des Miracles

Clochards under the Pont-Neuf. In the distance, the Pont des Arts (c. 1932).

The bum with his cat (c. 1932).

The dean of Parisian bums, Boulevard Saint-Jacques (c. 1934).

A Night with the Cesspool Cleaners

Cesspool cleaners, Rue Visconti, Saint-Germain-des-Prés (c. 1931).

Cesspool cleaners with their pump, Rue Rambuteau (c. 1931).

Cesspool cleaner directing the hose in the tank (c. 1931).

Supper with the cesspool cleaners, Saint-Paul district (c. 1931).

The Urinals of Paris

A urinal on the Boulevard Saint-Jacques (c. 1932).

A urinal, Boulevard Auguste-Blanqui (c. 1935).

The Underworld
The Police

Members of Big Albert's Gang, Place d'Italie (c. 1932).

Police during a raid in Montmartre (c. 1931).

Big Albert's Gang, Place d'Italie (c. 1931).

The Escaped Con

One of the oldest police stations, at the corner of the Rue de la Huchette and the Rue du Chat-qui-Pêche (c. 1932).

The wall of the Santé prison, Boulevard Arago (c. 1932). It was here that executions took place in 1939.

The escaped con one evening on the Rue de la Ferronnerie, in Les Halles (c. 1932).

Young toughs in a bistro near the Place d'Italie (c. 1932).

Lovers

Pair of lovers, Rue Croulebarbe, near the Place d'Italie (c. 1932).

(Clockwise from top left) Lovers in the park on the Champs-Elysées (c. 1932); Lovers on a bench, Boulevard Saint-Jacques, next to a bum (c. 1932); Lovers in a bistro, Rue Saint-Denis (c. 1931); Pair of Lovers, Place d'Italie (c. 1932).

Lovers, Place d'Italie (c. 1932).

The Bals-Musette

A bar, Rue de Lappe (c. 1932).

(Above) The band at the Bal de la Montagne Sainte-Geneviève (c. 1932); (below) The Bal des Quatre Saisons, Rue de Lappe (c. 1932).

Group of men at the bar of a bistro, Rue de Lappe (c. 1932).

Women with spit curls at the bar of a bistro, Rue de Lappe (c. 1932).

(Clockwise from top left) Couple in a bar, Rue Saint-Denis (c. 1931); Couple at the Bal des Quatre Saisons, Rue de Lappe (c. 1932); Couple at a bar, Rue de Lappe (c. 1933); Lovers' quarrel, Bal des Quatre Saisons, Rue de Lappe (c. 1932).

A happy group at the Quatre Saisons (c. 1932).

A prostitute playing Russian billiards, Boulevard Rochechouart, Montmartre (c. 1932).

Prostitutes in a bar, Boulevard Rochechouart, Montmartre (c. 1932).

Miss Diamonds

Miss Diamonds in the Bar de la Lune, Montmartre (c. 1932).

Miss Diamonds, Bar de la Lune, Montmartre (c. 1932).

Ladies of the Evening

A lady of the evening, Rue de Lappe (c. 1932).

Streetwalker near the Place d'Italie (c. 1932).

The same, from behind.

Two girls looking for tricks, Boulevard Montparnasse (c. 1931).

(Clockwise from top left) A girl in Les Halles, Rue de la Reynie, near the Boulevard Sébastopol (c. 1931); Streetwalker, Rue Quincampoix (c. 1932); A girl on the Rue Quincampoix, in carpet slippers, naked under her coat (c. 1932); A novice prostitute, Place d'Italie (c. 1932).

A lady of the evening near the Place d'Italie, in her spring finery (c. 1931).

A brothel in the Rue des Lombards. Boccaccio, author of **The Decameron**, was born on this street (c. 1932).

"Houses of Illusion"

The Rue Quincampoix and its **hôtels de passe** (c. 1932).

(Clockwise from top left) An avant-garde brothel, Porte Saint-Denis (c. 1931); The Japonaise (near Les Halles) (c. 1932); A pickup, near Les Halles (c. 1932); A pickup, near Les Halles (c. 1932).

Washing up in a brothel, Rue Quincampoix (c. 1932).

At Suzy, Rue Grégoire-de-Tours, in the Saint-Germain quarter (c. 1932).

Mirrored wardrobe in a brothel, Rue Quincampoix (c. 1932).

Suzy

Suzy, Rue Grégoire-de-Tours (c. 1932).

Waiting for clients (c. 1932).

"Madame" (c. 1932).

At Suzy (c. 1932).

At Suzy, introductions (c. 1932).

A monastic brothel, Rue Monsieur-le-Prince, Quartier Latin (c. 1931).

Artists' Dances in Montparnasse

(Above) Café terrace, the Dôme in Montparnasse (c. 1932); (below) A cab in front of the Dôme (1932).

"The Horde" at the Bal Bullier, Montparnasse (c. 1932).

(Above) Choosing the most beautiful model, "The Horde" (c. 1932); (below) "The Pantheress" with the band, "The Horde" at the Bal Bullier, Montparnasse (c. 1932).

The Bal Nègre in the Rue Blomet

Couple at the Bal Nègre, Rue Blomet (c. 1932).

Gisèle performing at the Boule Blanche in Montparnasse (c. 1931).

At the Cabane Cubaine in Montmartre (c. 1932).

Kiki of Montparnasse

Kiki surrounded with men at the Cabaret des Fleurs, Rue de Montparnasse (c. 1932).

Kiki with her accordion player at the Cabaret des Fleurs, Rue de Montparnasse (c. 1932).

Kiki with her friends Thérèse Treize de Caro and Lily (c. 1932).

In the Wings at the Folies-Bergère

An English girl in her dressing room at the Folies-Bergère (c. 1932).

A costumed showgirl, Folies-Bergère (c. 1932).

English girls in the dressing room, Folies-Bergère (c. 1932).

"The Rainbow" at the Folies-Bergère (c. 1932).

"Juan-les-Pins," Folies-Bergère (c. 1932).

"The Spider Web," Folies-Bergère (c. 1932).

The "Cage of Wild Beasts," Folies-Bergère (c. 1932).

View down onto the stage, Folies-Bergère (c. 1932).

The fire brigade, Folies-Bergère (c. 1932).

The Bal des Quat'z Arts

The Bal des Quat'z Arts. A couple getting "dressed" (c. 1931).

Leaving the Ecole des Beaux-Arts (c. 1931).

(Clockwise from top left) "Savages" in the Rue Bonaparte (c. 1931); "Savages" in the Rue Bonaparte (c. 1931); A gilded warrior (c. 1931–32); Gilded warriors (c. 1931–32).

Sodom and Gomorrah

Le Monocle

At Le Monocle, Boulevard Edgar-Quinet, Montparnasse (c. 1932).

A couple at Le Monocle (c. 1932).

Young female invert, Le Monocle (c. 1932).

Young female invert, Le Monocle (c. 1932).

Le Monocle, the bar. On the left is Lulu de Montparnasse (c. 1932).

The Ball at "Magic City"

Homosexual ball at Magic City, Rue Cognacq-Jay (c. 1932).

Homosexual ball at Magic City, Rue Cognacq-Jay (c. 1932).

"Duchess Zoé," the Ball at Magic City (c. 1932).

The Bal de la Montagne Sainte-Geneviève

The Bal de la Montagne Sainte-Geneviève (c. 1931).

Young couple wearing a two-in-one suit at the Bal de la Montagne Sainte-Geneviève (c. 1931).

A couple at the homosexual ball at Magic City (c. 1932).

A couple of butchers, Bal de la Montagne Sainte-Geneviève (c. 1931).

Young couple, Bal de la Montagne Sainte-Geneviève (c. 1931).

Mardi Gras at the Bal de la Montagne Sainte-Geneviève (c. 1931).

An Opium Den

An opium den, Avenue Bosquet. A tray with pipes, pins, oil lamp (c. 1931).

Smokers preparing their pipes (c. 1931).

A female habituée (c. 1931).

An opium smoker asleep (c. 1931).

M. B. in a gold brocade kimono (c. 1931).

A gas company employee extinguishing one of the last remaining gaslights, Boulevard Edgar-Quinet (c. 1931).